WHEN YOU COMIN BACK, RED RYDER?

HOME MOVIE
A Preface

A scene from the New York production.

WHEN YOU COMIN BACK,

BY

JAMES T. WHITE & COMPANY

RED RYDER?

MARK MEDOFF

CLIFTON, NEW JERSEY

Lines from *Mrs. Robinson*
© 1968 Paul Simon
Used with permission of the publisher.

Library of Congress Cataloging in Publication Data

Medoff, Mark Howard.
    When you comin back, Red Ryder?

    A play.
    I. Title.
PS3563.E27W48 1975   812'.5'4   74-28316
ISBN 0-88371-009-9
ISBN 0-88371-010-2 pbk.

Designed by Janet Anderson

Manufactured in the United States of America

HOME MOVIE

It has been a long time since I have been afraid of anything but madmen with guns. The rest, however threatening, can be challenged and dealt with.

In 1948 I am eight, my brother six, and—though twenty-six years later when I remind him he will not remember—we meet the Durango Kid for the first time at the Airway Theater in Louisville. I remember the Kid as the Superman of cowboys, changing his clothes in a cave rather than a cramped phone booth or closet. A mild mannered rancher until trouble hits, the Kid then transmogrifies into a scourge in black mask and tight black togs who rides a white horse to ninety minutes of rectified wrongs. He is accompanied on the road to righteousness by the loyal, if porcine and unresplendent, Smiley Burnett. All those top boys of yore, it seems, are companioned by another guy, and inevitably that other guy is afflicted with a pox, ranging from obesity (Pancho) to age (Gabby Hayes), from the curse of grunting American Indianhood (Tonto, Little Beaver) to imbecility (Pat Brady, who talks to Jeeps).

Nevertheless, I believe in the Durango Kid, as I come to believe in Cisco and Red and all the others. I'm not concerned that my heroes surround themselves with lepers and idiots, that they seem to have an abiding lack of interest in women—except as objects to save from other guys—or that their lives are as simply and cleanly plotted as my own. The Saturday matinee is an institution of my childhood, a schoolroom as surely as the one I attend at I. M. Bloom School Monday through Friday. My brother and I learn about justice and reenact what we learn in back of our apartment. We charge down the hill on our bikes, I the Durango Kid, the principal player (and to this day I cannot stand it otherwise), my brother and our cronies my assistants—pedaling hell-bent-for-leather to the rescue of a girl whose name I cannot remember, from whom I accept a brief thank you for all of us, if I am feeling beneficent, before leading my forces off to gun down her defilers with loaded fingers or cap pistols.

Why would I suspect then, when I am eight, that when I return to Louisville for the first time in twenty-five years the Airway Theater will house a furnace company?

5

It was August 1, 1971, and I was thirty-one, disillusioned of my ideals into compatible rage and equanimity. (I imagined a scenario in which TIME or *Newsweek* did a cover story on me entitled "The Marriage of Genius and Rage." Nice.) My wife Stephanie and I entered a Toddle House in Albuquerque out of nostalgia: I remembered my father telling me when I was a boy that Toddle Houses served up terrific eggs.

We were in Albuquerque to see two one-act plays I'd written. It was to have been three, but the director couldn't flush out an actor who was willing at one point to put his hands to his groin and squeeze his own genitalia. I had been trying with kamikaze concentration to write not merely good plays, but a Good play. Neither of the two we were to see (or the pariah third) was better than good. Sometimes I drove myself to such artistic frustration that I believed I *should* have become a doctor. I would have today been in practice with my father in Miami, young Dr. Medoff rather than Assistant Professor of English Medoff, one of New Mexico's most minor writers.

We found ourselves alone in the diner with two kids in the last of their teens—an obese waitress and a greasy twig of a boy who had worked the night shift and lingered now to play his part in an illusive love affair with her.

I am nine, writing my first book. It is about a boy and a donkey and is based on the hardbound volume sitting in front of me. I am changing conjunctions.

A crippled young man came into the Toddle House, sat in a booth, read his newspaper.

Stephen and Nancy—their names—continued their tender, abusive dance.

I was sure that they were a play about themselves. I told Stephanie to remember what she could.

As for the eggs . . . the stench of the Drano in the stopped-up sink directly under our noses took care of that. So much for nostalgia.

When I am fifteen my beloved Dodgers beat the goddamn Yankees in the World Series at last, healing the stigmata of those earlier wounds. Around World Series time my tenth grade English teacher has his classes write a short story. Mine is about a teenager who kills someone and goes to prison. (I can only conjecture at how much the domination of the Yankees over the Dodgers in my boyhood and early teens has to do with the development of my obdurate hostility toward anything that seeks to dominate me.) My story is called "He Was Only A Kid." I receive an A+ on it. The teacher tells the class he has never given an A+ on anything before and he asks me to read the story to the class. I am, perhaps, never prouder in my life.

He instructs me to send the story to COLLIERS . . . *which sends it back with blinding speed. Bastards! I had typed "Age 15" right there on the title page—some second string reader could have at least written a little encouragement on the lousy standard rejection form. ("Dear Master Medoff: Whew!—what a story. I'm afraid, however, it doesn't* QUITE *fit our present needs." Should have sent the damn thing to* ARGOSY *anyway.)*

Reeling from the agony of that rejection, I become a closet writer, turning out the stuff in my room at night and stashing it under my stroke books and SPORT *magazines in the closet.*

Usually we made the two hundred and twenty-five mile drive from Albuquerque to Las Cruces, where we lived, in three hours, sometimes a minute or two under. We had an old Porsche C then which we loved to drive fast around corners and down highways. It took longer that morning because Stephanie wrote on the *Parade* section of Sunday's Albuquerque *Journal* everything we could remember about the two kids in the Toddle House and what they had to say to each other.

I am seventeen and, in my main public occupation, a jock—although one who will never fulfill his dream of quarterbacking the University of Miami Hurricanes on the floor of the Orange Bowl, a failure I will never quite forgive myself. Because I am an athlete and a member of Student Council, I figure I won't be bombed with cries of "Fairy!" if I submit a short story to the Embryo, *the literary magazine at Miami Beach High School. The faculty advisor tells me it's a fine story but that he wonders if my mother or father has not written it with me.*

I dive headlong back into the closet.

Armed hungrily with the notes on the Albuquerque *Journal Parade* section, I sat down the next morning to write a one act play about a greasy counterman named Stephen Castle and a fat waitress named Nancy. They worked in a rundown diner in a small town in my mind somewhere between Deming and

Lordsburg, N. M. By the time I had finished the one act play the next day, the young crippled man who read his newspaper had become a crippled man in his sixties who owned a motel and service station next door and Stephanie and I had become a textile importer and his wife. She, oddly, came out of my head carrying a Guarnerius violin.

An Interstate by-pass has opened. Hints of things dying under the heels of "progress."

The play ended with Stephen Castle walking out of the diner with the importer and his wife. They were going to drive him on the new superhighway to Baton Rouge; there, he insisted, he had a great future in a restaurant where the waiters wore tuxedos. . . . He returned moments later, unable to make the break.

Or not permitted to by the playwright.

In my freshman year at the University of Miami I am taking Advanced Comp from an elderly, distant woman named Dr. Grace Garlinghouse-King. I'm bored with writing advanced compositions and with almost everything else. I ask her if I may write a short story. I can't read what she thinks of my request or of me. She gives me A's on my advanced compositions—perhaps she has suspected me all along of something like this.

The play about Stephen and Nancy was about more than whether or not a nineteen year old boy broke away from a life leading nowhere, but I didn't happen to know what else it wanted to deal with. Confused, I put the play away and wouldn't touch it, as it happened, for a year. When I returned to it, a number of my demons synthesized in the character of Teddy, who walked into that diner and exhumed and buried bodies of my child- and young manhood, blessing me with the purgation of glorious and bitter tears for the six days it took to draft the whole play.

I was never happier with the experience of *Red Ryder* (or *Ryder* as, I'm told, it's known in the theatrical lexicon of New York) than I was during those six days. It is the dizzying intimacy of discovering a play in my own head in the privacy of my own den that is orgasmic. The rest—the collaboration, the business of Show Biz, the audiences—about all of that

8

there is something else, steeped in a terrible and delicious ambivalence.

At two in the morning several days after I have given her a short story called "One Blind Mouse" (in this one two guys kill six people), Dr. Grace Garlinghouse-King awakens me to say that there is nothing more she can teach me about writing. It is an extraordinary thing for her to say to someone desperately in the market for words even half as strong. She has awakened the man who teaches Creative Writing at the University of Miami, she tells me, a man of local legend named Fred Shaw, and I am to see him that afternoon. He will have read my story by then. If he feels as strongly as she about my prospects, I will do my time in her class writing for him.

January, 1972. Gloria in Excelsis: My first play, *The Wager*, was to be done at the HB Playwrights Foundation Theatre in Greenwich Village. Greenwich Village—that place of mythic proportions I dreamed of being a dissipated part of in my quaintly, safely rebellious college days. Something called an Equity Showcase. Also something called a miracle.

I had known from the beginning that Albuquerque and Denver, San Antonio, Palo Alto, and Las Cruces meant nothing until you had been in New York City. (The Apocrypha have not endured the ages because they are apocryphal.) But how in hell did a lad writing plays in Las Cruces, N.M., get someone in New York City to do anything about his work, other than, say, ignore it.

Some of our local cognoscenti assured me that what I needed was an agent. But that, on the other hand, most agents—your top boys—wouldn't touch you until you'd "done something." *But* that, on the other hand, nobody would "do anything" unless you had an agent. All of the "on the other hands" struck me as ballbreakers.

Others who knew as little as I said I had to move to New York and "go see people." Move to New York? Did they have any idea how long it would take me to work myself into a starting quarterback slot in those Central Park games that have been going on for years!

My dentist in Miami Beach, a friend since childhood, kept sticking his fingers into my mouth and telling me to write to his cousin Kenneth from Cleveland, who was "in the theater."

9

I was cynical and frightened; I, who had "heard stories" and read *The Season*, scoffed at my dentist: Everybody knew somebody "in the theater." Dr. Marchand should keep his cousin to himself and stick to teeth!

I was a desperate man. Past thirty now and no more than a whisper of my *least* acceptable literary intentions. A wagon train of suicide notes rolled through my fantasies of failure as I sat at my stool each morning before I launched another attack against my demons.

I had to get rolling!

All right. I sent my dentist's cousin *The Wager*. If, as I was sure, he was merely another poseur, who would be the wiser? Four days after Cousin Kenneth should have received the manuscript in Cleveland I received a telegram from New York. (I had an unlisted phone number, not in preparation for my eventual fame, but so that my first wife could not call me.) As Stephanie and I drove down to the Western Union office, I said theatrically to this beautiful woman I felt compelled to become immortal for and whom I would shortly marry for Love: "This is it!"

The telegram said that Cousin Kenneth could do an immediate reading production of *The Wager*. The telegram said to call him. I did and he and I were wed in an extension of the old mail order bride routine: immaculate conception. We were pregnant.

"Tell us, Mr. Medoff, what is your advice to the young playwright?" "Have your teeth cleaned regularly."

I spent three and a half years writing stories and a "novel" for Fred Shaw. Master of prolepsis, he prescribes a ten year apprenticeship to discipline and dedication. He flagellates and strokes me. He is, next to my father and a head counselor at the camp my brother and I attended through most of the fifties, the only "real" man I ever love and respect. Real in the sense that there were others, not real but "heroic" in the tradition of the American myth that died its grotesque death in the late sixties when our revolution failed utterly, punctuated for emphasis by the third coming of Richard Nixon. "Heroes" like the glorious Duke of Flatbush, Cousy of the behind the back lay-up, Ike of the "good" war, and corrals full of clean livin cowboys who straightened up more little towns and

10

Sodomites than even the America of myth could have cast. Finally, JFK and Sandy Koufax there for a while. But about JFK there were the nagging rumors of inconstancy; of Sandy . . . well, what can one say intelligently about the paradoxical lunacy of arthritis of the elbow?

Fred Shaw helps me to learn to write, for he tells me in absolute humility, I think, that no one can teach me. Read and write, he admonishes me, and through those three and a half years I do very little else. I am, for the first time in my life, committed fully to something at which I might fail.

A year and a half before The Wager was to get its HB production, Ken Frankel did a reading production of the play at The Cubiculo. I couldn't afford to be there. He told me that the powers at The Cubiculo said it was the best reading production they'd seen there and they were definitely interested in the play. My friend Top Cat saw it, said the reading production stank and that the play had been injudiciously cut to fill a prescribed space. Tie game, end of nine.

Ken wanted to show the play to a New York Producer he used to work for, a man with many Big Productions under his belt. I'd never heard of him, but that was certainly no criterion of anything except that he wasn't David Merrick, whom I had heard of.

The New York Producer liked the play but wanted to see it done somewhere before he "optioned" it. (An option agreement is a form of chattel enslavement of a "property" for a period of months—usually six—set down in an elaborate denigration of the English language. Decoded, the option agreement buys the right to *consider* doing a play.)

Incredible. Just like that and I was mere baby steps away from being The Toast of Broadway. I began working up some snappy patter so that I could give as good as I got the first time the old Carsoni dragged me onto The Tonight Show.

I arranged to have the play done in Miami. Ken would direct. I would take a leave of absence from the university. Stephanie would move with her daughter into my house to care for my son the dog. Her daughter and my dog were the same age. Perfect. This was it.

Ken backed out of leaving his job for certain glory at the last minute. The hell with him! I wanted to direct the play myself anyway. It got rave notices in a town infamous for its wholesale slaughter of and malignant indifference to theater. The play ran three months and earned me in excess of a hundred dollars. Deducted from my air fare, living expenses, and the salary I had given up at the university, getting the New York Producer a "look" at my play ran me about six grand.

My mother, father, and brother were delighted though. And I got to lord it over some of my former classmates who were already trudging into the obsequies of their medical and legal practices. The New York Producer was impressed . . . but wanted just *one more* free look at the play before he optioned it. Can't be too careful, what with blah blah blah. Okay. Anything.

A mere year later, the play was done at HB through an arrangement the New York Producer set up with the Foundation, for which I will pay henceforward two percent of my earnings on that play. A careful man, that New York Producer, and one who knew the value of my dollar. But what matter? This was it!

The experience at HB, for our first "professional" outing, was infinitely rewarding to both Stephanie and me. We cared deeply for the people involved in the production. We were totally enamored of "New York Theater," *real theater* . . . despite the fact that the New York Producer disliked the production. He still "loved" the play, however, and decided to definitely option it for Off-Broadway production next fall (Jesus, Off-Broadway! This was it!) . . . *following* just ONE MORE FREE LOOK at the "property" at a place called The Manhattan Theatre Club (fleeting visions of hors d'oeuvres being served by a couple of natty old geezers in tattersall vests to a lot of chic New York theater types). "Important tests," said the N. Y. Producer. "Blah blah blah ensemble. Best to be sure that blah blah blah." I was beginning to suffer attacks of what must have been aphasia. No, no! My educated wife and I battled our distrust of the man gallantly, rationalized brilliantly . . . for, on the very brink of *certain* glory, we saw no present alternative to him. And we were, if nothing else at that point, pragmatists to the core.

To compound the-alternative-to-him-that-I-didn't-see theory, I told the N. Y. P. that I had just finished two other plays: One, *The Kramer*, I had just been informed would be done immediately by the American Conservatory Theatre in San Francisco in their new Plays in Progress series on a grant from the Office for Advanced Drama Research, one of those wonderful but maddeningly rare organizations that gives a damn about new writers; the other play, however, called *When You Comin Back, Red Ryder?*, was more or less just sitting around waiting to become the object of further prevarication.

He read it and told me it would never make it as a play. Make a helluva movie, he told me. I was tempted—the house in Bell Air, the pool, Dalmatians, Cy DeVore shirts. . . . I said no, though. I wrote it as a play, I said, and I wanted to try to get it done that way. Foolish, he told me. Come on, whudduya say, let him see if he couldn't find a buyer in television.

Television! That did it. I was too young and far too egotistical to imagine I could write anything inconsequential enough that my only option for it would be television.

Appear at this point Variation II of the dentist with the cousin "in the theater": One of my writing students at New Mexico State University had an aunt who was "in the theater" in New York. I called her. I knew well enough now not to look a gift aunt in the mouth. She was doing sets for a little theater group "uptown" called The Circle Repertory Theater and was playing a bit part in the play they currently had in rehearsal, called *The Hot L Baltimore.*

I met her. She was gracious as all hell and took me to the Circle, there introduced me to the young man in charge, Marshall Mason. He said he would be glad to read my script and that he would try to get someone down to see *The Wager.*

I told him that I'd send the script up with a friend of mine who was anxious to direct it, fella name a Frankel who went to Northwestern when Marshall was there. (Some aphorist told me back about then that there were only ten people in Show Business and if you knew three of them, you'd work forever.)

The summer I graduate college, I park cars in New Rochelle and sell hot dogs at a carnival in Ottawa. I am still under the fringe influence of Jack Kerouac and those boys. Part of me yearns to suffer in filth and squalor, to endure my disaffection in the manner of those wonderful derelicts in On the Road. *I am stymied hopelessly, however, by the Jewish Cleanliness Fetish. I am aimless, though, in the sense that I am armed with no*

13

"acceptable" direction to my life. My aimlessness, on the other hand, is slightly complicated by the fact that I want to make a decent living while I wander about "committing experience" (as I enjoyed referring to it) and continuing my quest for literary brilliance. My mother and father are trying to be adult about the whole thing but are terrified. A BA in English, they have counseled me since I gave up pre-med, is worthless. I do not tell them that I agree . . . or that I am terrified too.

When I am in Ottawa, my mother sends me a telegram telling me that I am one of the winners in the Prize College Stories 1963 contest and that Random House will publish my story in the fall. In HARDBACK.

A heretofore studiously undemonstrative-when-happy individual, I run screaming through the Central Canadian Exhibition, a lunatical ombudsman for The Young Writer With Only A BA In English.

At the end of the summer I land in Washington, D. C., as Assistant Director of Admissions at a technical institute. I envision that I will work at the institute by day, write by night, and within a year or so be rich and famous and playing quarterback for the Kennedys on the weekends.

Ken called to say that Marshall loved Red Ryder and that we could do a workshop of the play at the Circle in June. If that went well, they'd open their next season with it.

I was commuting between San Francisco and Las Cruces for The Kramer.

The New York Producer caught me in San Francisco, told me CBS had given him the go ahead to negotiate with me for the T.V. rights to Red Ryder. They wanted to make a Movie of the Week out of it. I would write the screenplay. The N. Y. P. waited expectantly for me to be tickled to death. He was not happy that I was not. He told me what I needed was the advice of a good agent—whose advice, I could only presume, would be to accept the grand offices of the N. Y. P.—so he had interested the best he knew in me via The Wager. Gilbert Parker and I talked on the phone. He was Vice-President of something called Curtis-Brown Ltd., which sounded suspiciously like a conservative haberdashery, but no matter. I liked him immediately. I liked him even more when he advised me to hold onto all the rights to Red Ryder and do it the way I wanted.

14

I spend a year and a half with the technical institute in Washington. The closest I come to quarterbacking for the Kennedys is a glimpse one Sunday of the President and his wife walking across the Ellipse a couple of months before time changes in America.

As for rich and famous . . . The institute creates the position of Supervisor of Publications for me. I put out five enormously irrelevant publications for the place and coach the basketball team to an 0-7 record in the City League. I get even with the basketball team for its misuse of my advice by leading the staff team to a 60 point victory over the uncoordinated bastards in the first—and last—Student-Staff game. All of their girl friends and wives are there. I feel some better.

In March, the team in a sense gets even with me when a kid driving for a liquor store drives his car through the driver's side of mine with me in it. I go home to Miami Beach and into the hospital to see if anyone can figure out how to get rid of this headache I have for three months.

In September I enter graduate school at Stanford, aiming at another "worthless" degree in English. I have not dealt well with the Real World. Do not like it. I am relieved to go back to school for two years—to that sanctuary and safety.

In May, 1973, following a surprisingly unromantic operation on my aging-jock left knee, I whipped to N. Y. for a weekend to hear the first reading of *Red Ryder*. "Whipping" here and there was giving me the sanctimonious feeling that I was much hotter spit than I was. Of the eight people who read that Saturday, two—Brad Dourif and Jim Kiernan—went all the way with us. (Over a year later, Jim and I would stand backstage at the Eastside Playhouse, as the play moved toward its three hundredth performance and I got ready to do my last performance as Teddy, and we would marvel at all of it before we parted and before it ended.)

I met my agent for the first time that day. He was shaped differently than I expected. He sounded shorter on the telephone, was in fact a big guy, sharp dresser, smoker of an obscure brand of cigarettes that lent him an appealing esoteric quality. I was to learn as time went on and he negotiated large pieces of my life that he was, as we used to say, "tough as nails." The New York Producer regretted many times, I suspect, ever bringing me together with him. That first day, most notably, Gilbert told me he wasn't sure the play would work and he introduced me to the spinach, mushroom, and bacon salad, a confection I couldn't fathom having lived without for thirty-two years.

In two years at Stanford I write nothing of value. I remember myself best as someone who accomplishes a year of sincere tennis (the first year) and a year of colitis and psychotherapy (the second). (Anyone who claims to have seen everything there is to see and done everything there is to do but hasn't had colitis is full of crap—Old Confucian proverb.)

I am a gaunt neurotic on the fringe of the revolution that is exploding at Berkeley and sort of festooning at Stanford. As outraged by the war as anyone, I am uninterested in auditioning for the show as all the choice roles seem taken. Or perhaps I am merely afflicted with stage fright.

For my thesis, I write a novel called The Savior. *It has a lot to do with my mind's-eye vision of myself as a bad-faith Christ. It is accepted by the Writing Center faculty. However, as I am well aware that it stinks, I assume they are too. I am too busy to care. I am obsessed, as is Bellow's Henderson, with that voice in me that cries I want, I want. I want to be a "successful" writer; enough getting ready! I want to be immortal! I want to be able to stomach myself! I want to stop having to eat mashed potatoes every day to help the medication I am taking to stop me from shitting my brains out! My hands and knuckles are bruised and scabbed from the punches I unload on the bathroom door. I punish my hands for the tricks my mind is playing on my gastrointestinal system. Makes sense.*

I want to go to Europe in May when I finish at Stanford. My psychiatrist doesn't seem to think it's a terrific idea but I'm angry at him for helping to make me better by inviting me to experience a lot of truths that make me sick. My parents think I'm planning to freeload the rest of my life and think I ought to get a job and cut the crap (Love to!). But I'm angry at them too because (Who else but!) they're at the root of what I'm trying to get better from that's making me sick. Fred Shaw, however, at whom I am angry only because I have not written a thing of note, tells me flatly that what I should do is take a teaching position somewhere and Persevere. I know I should take a teaching position, goddamn it, but because I know it I

16

don't want to! It is the end of April, I protest, surely it's too late to find a teaching position for next year. He tells me to write to a friend of his who is Head of the English Department at New Mexico State University, the school at which he had begun his teaching career years before.

I go through Las Cruces on my way from Palo Alto to Miami Beach. It is brutally hot and I am driving an un-air conditioned black Volkswagen that continues to vapor lock at regular intervals. I am traveling with the girl who has suffered through my colitis and my psychotherapy with me and whom I am rewarding for her loyalty by tormenting toward madness.

New Mexico State University strikes me on sight as a monument to Demeter, the goddess of agriculture, sculptured in manure. It has cows, for chrissake, right on campus. I am a Jewish boy from Miami Beach, what the hell do I want with cows! I swear a secret oath to myself after having peach cobbler with the Head and his wife: Unlike that great man of my childhood, I shall not return. No sir!

I spend the first several weeks at home looking for another job. Am offered a teaching position at the Hebrew Academy on the Beach but turn it down on the grounds that I could not possibly wear a yarmulka to class every day. I come, though, within an exhalation of breath ("Yes.") of accepting a job with the Peace Corps as the writer/researcher on a psychiatric team. It's a six month job, from which I can save three thousand dollars to go to Europe and find Sartre and make him explain the predicament he and I have gotten me into. Maybe the Peace Corps Newsletter will publish a few of my stories. I think constantly of having turned one way instead of another, and how very different things might have been, would almost certainly have been, and I am enraptured and infuriated by the sense and senselessness of it all.

In August I pack up and head back to Las Cruces. My first day there I go into a Seven/Eleven store, browse over the paperback rack and am just about to steal a book—a business I honed to a fine science in graduate school—when it comes to me out of the burning bush of my brain that I am twenty-six years old and an Instructor of English at a university, that suddenly I am an adult in some vague technical sense, and that a whole era of my life is irremediably over.

I have been here eight years now. I have not stolen a book.

17

Nor, for that matter, have I had an attack of colitis.

The first rehearsal Gilbert and I saw of *Red Ryder* as it was being prepared for its week long workshop run was a remarkable experience. In short, we were appalled. In long, we were terrified the play was going to meet an undeservedly gruesome stillbirth. I could barely speak to Ken. Gilbert left immediately after the rehearsal without bothering even the "barely" part. The play had been in rehearsal two weeks and made its run in another week. I could not imagine anything but embarrassment. The staging seemed inept, some of the casting improbable, and to my own glaring discredit, the crucial scene in the second act between the husband and wife sucked.

I had been floating on a wave of tenuous elation for months—since *The Wager* at HB and *The Kramer* at ACT; I had *really* begun to think this was it.

That one rehearsal was a lung and a half of water and a stomach knotting reaffirmation of my obsessive unwillingness to allow others to control my destiny. It is a problematical obsession in the theater.

I love teaching Freshman Composition. I expected at best to tolerate it. I am happy to get up every morning and go to class. I am a very good teacher and my students feed off of me. For years I will break into a sweat every time I walk into class—not from nervousness but from excitement. But I'm also lonely and not meeting girls who are not students (upholding for the moment the ethic that decrees against dating students). I live a monastic life away from the university my first few months. I have a small SONY: I lie on my couch with it on my chest. I do not like Las Cruces now any better than I did last summer. To Las Cruces, an Italian restaurant is a place that serves pizza and ravioli. People drive pick-ups with rifles racked in the back of the cabs. Some of the roads aren't even paved. My novel goes out to publishers; comes back. My year in therapy has not settled; I am erratic and hacking up my few new friends and lovers.

I keep writing though. If nothing else, I can martyr myself to myself, I figure. I begin a short story. The second day I sit down to it I realize on rereading that I have nine pages of dialogue inundating two lines of narrative. Although my mother has insisted for years that I should be writing plays, I decide to try turning the story into a play anyway (Ah, blessed Maturity. At last!). I call it The Wager.

The workshop production of *Red Ryder* opened. The audience at the first performance screamed and whistled. I was stunned: Were they crazy? I knew we'd made impressive headway, but there were things, I felt, for which Ken, the cast, and I were unpardonably guilty. But even Gilbert assured me that it "worked."

Reenter at this point the New York Producer, who owned for the hard won, really-not-that-exciting-anymore sum of two hundred and fifty dollars the option on *The Wager*. The joys of the Theater, I've found, seem always to come *at least* a month after you've earned them, thereby systematically mitigating your enjoyment of them. In dealing with this man, I found that his hesitancy to make a decision—or "carefulness," why don't we call it to give him the benefit of the doubt—his "carefulness" alleviated the initial rush of a promise time and again. The N. Y. P. said he was wrong about *Red Ryder*. The play "worked," he said. He wanted to option it *immediately*. I resisted both leaping for joy and for his throat.

He took Stephanie and me to Sardi's the next afternoon—our first visit there. We felt Show Biz as hell (no matter that we learned afterward we were in the schlock section, packed in with a bunch of rubbernecks who didn't realize they were in the schlock section either). He told us that he wanted to open *Red Ryder* in the fall and *The Wager* in the spring, convinced that *Red Ryder* would have the greater commercial appeal.

Our feelings for this man were very complicated by this time. We felt like young marrieds being hyped on—not life insurance —but snake oil or one of those other questionable elixirs. When we were with him, we couldn't help be attracted to something about him (and *still* find that to be true). When we viewed him from an objective distance, we would have preferred to cut his tongue out and serve it to the dogs outside the saloon.

Gilbert was adamant that I not option *Red Ryder* to the N. Y. P. He had had *The Wager* to deal with for over a year. It had taken him that long just to sign the piddling option agreement. We didn't need him to sit on *Red Ryder* too. We could hire a chicken.

I won't pretend I fully comprehend the perverse notion of

19

loyalty and who knows what else that led me to overrule Gilbert and allow the N. Y. P. to option *Red Ryder*. The play was *set* to open the Circle's season; the Circle was the hottest group in town because of *The Hot L*; if *Red Ryder* did well, any number of producers would be interested in moving the production to Off-Broadway. I have the silly feeling that I didn't want to "hurt" this man who coaxed me over a crock of cheese in Sardi's to give him this play when he had done nothing with the first. Perhaps if not the cut of his jib, the cut of his hair. He had a hair style that screamed of competence. Oh hell, I don't know.

The option was signed after weeks of maddening, niggling "carefulness" and a cross contract hacked out in flesh and bone with the Circle. I had a nightmare fantasy in which the play moved to Off-Broadway, under the aegis not of Zeus of course but of the N. Y. P., bearing not the head of Gorgon but a likeness of the Mad Hatter, a comic strip bubble coming out of his mouth crying, "I'm late, I'm late, I'm late."

And now the fun started. Ken, the N. Y. P., and the folks at Circle felt the cast could remain essentially as it was in the workshop for the opening at the end of October—for the "real" thing: a "Welcome to the American theater, Mr. Medoff" . . . or banishment back to the desert of New Mexico, there to draw flies to my carcass. No thanks. I wouldn't have it, and there ensued debate, the seriousness of which was mitigated by the grotesquely humorous undertones (a mere pair of syllables away from undertaker) inherent to dissecting absent human beings in their external roles (actor, writer, so forth). I insisted—as I finally pointed out it said right there in my contract I could—that three of the actors, including the lead, be recast. The N. Y. P., out of fear I think, and Marshall Mason, out of long distance reports, since he was in Los Angeles directing *Hot L* during our workshop run, concluded that I was crazy to want to break up a winning combination, that what "worked" should be left alone. I couldn't accept that line of thinking—my mind swings to "winning" teams made better, sometimes great by trades and the acquisition of new blood—and, aside from the distastefulness of having to hurt those three actors, I'm glad I couldn't.

The debate raged for months. Let's rejoin it later.

Ken came out to Las Cruces for a week. We ate a lot of

20

Mexican food in a lot of diners, worked on the script and on the directorial concept. (In another debate that was going on, pressure was being applied to me to replace him.) We worked sternly with each other. Parted confidently.

I returned to New York in late August on my way to Los Angeles where The Mark Taper Forum was going to do *The Kramer* in its "New Theatre for Now Festival." We began the task of recasting four of the cast—the fourth being Clarisse, the wife, because the actress who played her in the workshop had taken a position elsewhere. Most important, however, was the casting of the lead, Teddy.

Of the perhaps thirty young men we read for Teddy in those four days, only two seemed right to me, and one, Kevin Conway, seemed the righter of the two once I got past the fact that the other one looked more like the playwright. There was opposition to Kevin, however. Everyone agreed that he did a magnificent reading, that he was a wonderful young actor. The reluctance was based on other things, almost exclusively physical. (It is amusing to note that months later Kevin told me at lunch one day that one of the people involved in this casting fiasco had told him that it was I who opposed him because I didn't think he was sexy enough. Very clever, those Chinese.)

The wars that went on during the next three weeks, the compromises agreed to and backed out of by various factions, the jockeying for historical position . . . culminated with me in a pay phone booth in Westwood, California, and Ken and the N. Y. P. on extensions in the N. Y. P.'s office in New York. I was screaming at them in an apoplectic rage that I was going to make perfectly clear to them for the very last time that the young man who had played Teddy in the workshop—a nice young man, an attractive and talented young man—was *wrong* for the part and would play it over my dead body; that as far as I was concerned, we should have cast Kevin Conway three weeks ago; and that if they didn't go ahead and commit to him and get the goddamn play into rehearsal on time I was coming through the transcontinental wires and I was going to tear both of their tongues right out of their goddamn throats.

Now, deep down inside, I didn't expect my threats and hysteria to have the least affect on these men. But they did. Perhaps I had driven them to exhaustion. How foolish of me to have been trying to sway them with cool verbal imprecations.

Threats and hysteria. I'd remember that. They agreed to Kevin Conway.

Not the war, to be sure, but at least a notable skirmish.

The Wager, *when I finish it in early 1967, is a long one act play in ten scenes. It runs the two nights of the annual Ides of March Festival at the Las Cruces Community Theater. Mentally, I break a bottle of champagne across my bow and launch myself to sea. I have been sailing since.*

The other person who resides in my shell, the one who strives to live a "normal" life, gets married that September, largely, I think, to do penance for real and imagined sins he has committed against the women in his life. My wife directs my second play, another one act, Machinations, *at the next Ides of March Festival. The year after that it's* Doing a Good One for the Red Man, *which I direct.*

In those three years, I get an education in the basic theater as an actor, director, writer. I hesitate to wonder at the quality of life had there been no Las Cruces Community Theater crammed into a moldering adobe building in the old Mexican quarter. (I. O. U. one new theater.)

In the summer of 1969, Doing a Good One for the Red Man *is one of the "featured" plays at the New Playwrights Festival at Trinity University in San Antonio, sponsored by Trinity and the Dallas Theatre Center. Now, by this time I am as confident inside as I appear to be outside about my prospects as a playwright, so the being-chosen is merely another step in the progression toward rich and famous. What happens after the actual presentation of* Red Man *on the final night of the Festival is something else again.*

It is part of the dues for being chosen that following the doing the playwright shall come forward and face his audience, much in the tradition, let's say, of the defendant who is guilty until proven innocent. In the case of all the plays but mine and the one by Mark Berman, the other "featured" playwright, the facing of audiences takes place before the other members of the Festival—other novitiates, the actors, a few administrative types, among them a priest, schooled in gentleness. In Berman's and my cases, however, our audience consists not only of the above-mentioned, but of several hundred of San Antonio's wealthiest theatermakers (Remember the Alamo? They do.) and several *"famous" writers, with only one of whom I am even remotely familiar.*

Doing a Good One for the Red Man, *as it happens, is a farce about the white man and the Injun, dealt with as indelicately as possible. The audience in San Antonio that evening starts off laughing at the play, following their cue cards smartly. But then, maybe a third of the way through it, they stop. And don't start again. As Lenny says, "It's granite out there."*

I am not pleased to have to go up on stage with those "famous" writers after the last note of the dirge has hit leadenly in the house. The Playwright-from-Texas (a man whose claim to fame, as I recall, is a paean to Texas which is performed religiously each summer somewhere in Texas for bands of heathen tourists) says, and I summarize for him here, that he thinks the content of my play is a lot of commie horseshit and the language reeks. In short, I hit him right where he lives.

In the midst of the ensuing bloodletting, Paul Baker, Director of the Dallas Theatre Center and Head of the Trinity Drama Department, feels compelled to come on stage to remind the audience that the discussion of the play is supposed to be constructive and that the viewpoint should be theatrical rather than political—for, in fact, the "discussion" has turned to disabusing me of my notion that the white man has done quite a number on the ole Injun—at least these white Texas folks didn't have nothin to do with it. We're the good *white folks, boy. It was you Jewish people put up all them pawnshops on them reservations.*

As the dust settles during the next few hours, I experience as powerful a high from the upset I've created as I would had those people leaped in sympathy to their feet at the end of the performance.

I aggravate the hell out of people in real life, why not in the theater? Rhetorical question, of course.

On October 30, 1973, *When You Comin Back, Red Ryder?* opened at the Circle, Stephanie and Gilbert watched. Ken and I did not. Afterward, a party on stage followed by a pilgrimage to Sardi's to await Mel Gussow's review in *The New York Times.* ("He looked pissed when he left.") Ken and I wear the same calm exterior underlaid with fatalistic hatred.

The early edition arrived, brought to the table in the tradition of the Theater by the maitre d'. The papers were practically torn open. So long, calm exterior.

There was no review. How embarrassing! And here again, the loathsome business of having your destiny in the hands of others. The memory leaves the taste of something fetid in my mind even today. (This build to nothing is not unlike what happened little more than a month later when, on opening night at the Eastside Playhouse, Kevin reached the climactic moment of the first act, pulled the trigger, and the gun did not fire.)

(We labor to drive our lives to climactic trigger-pullings, and misfires, if you ask me, are a real pain in the ass.)

We disbanded. The *Daily News* was on strike, so there would be nothing from Douglas Watt until the strike was settled—and just as well, it turned out.

The next day, Ken and his roommate, Jacqueline, Stephanie and I drove into Connecticut, trying to keep busy while we waited for Mel Gussow, for the AP, and the suburban papers which, we were assured by someone we assumed didn't know what he was talking about, would be forthcoming beginning at eventide.

It was a day for reflection. Whatever doubts Ken ever had about the play, whatever doubts I had about his direction, we had worked creatively together through hours and days of script and production problems, had worked to a bond of brotherhood, not a relationship without rancor but one strong in empathy and blood. We were proud of what we had wrought together, proud of our cast; and we would know tomorrow, whatever the outcome of the notices, that we had given it a good shot. We reflected on the efficacy of workshop productions—the wonder of the opportunity to "work out" a play relatively inexpensively before a bunch of blessed loonies gambled fifty-sixty thousand dollars on an Off-Broadway production, more on a Broadway job. It was a day for feeling familial, protectively smug, and insular.

We ate at a wonderful restaurant on a little stream in Westport and drove back into the city. It was midnight when I got out of the silent car to buy *The Times* at Seventy-second and Broadway. I turned coolly to the index in the second section and read "Circle Theatre does it again." I didn't bother to turn to the review before I raised my fist in the air in a gesture of defiance and trotted across the intersection, a primal scream upon my lips.

The year I come up for tenure at the university, the revolution is dead, the war continues, and two of my colleagues decide to have my tenure denied and, in effect, bring about my firing. The grounds they choose are simple: I am a communist and teach a straight Marxist line in my classes, failing any students who don't adhere to the line. Marvelous!

The essence of the problem, really, is perhaps not so much more than this: I come into "their" department, a rakish, slightly mad young man who, because he has difficulty respecting anyone, does not respect them for a perfectly plausible reason—they simply don't strike him as other than ordinary—and therefore he is in no way deferential toward them. How many people, after all, are worthy of deference?

Several of my colleagues—hardly deferential types themselves—come to my defense with my department head—a confirmed liberal straining at the administrative bit—and after months of details, accusations, and a goodly portion of dated McCarthy clichés, the vote of the Tenure and Promotion Committee is 7-2, my favor. As for my two accusers, one retires quietly, an old warhorse limping off to the seaside in California; the other continues in withered silence, both of them, I expect, eating their livers by the hunk over the developments in my life the past several years. Bon appétit, *boys.*

The Gussow review in hand, others passed to us verbally, Ken, Jacque, Stephanie, and I made several hundred dollars' worth of hyperbolic phone calls from the Medoffs' hotel room, our lives changing even as we spoke.

Though I have the year before San Antonio expanded The Wager *into a full length play and it has been done twice by* The Stanford Repertory Theatre, The Trial of Myles Fife, *based on my tenure experience, is the first play I intend from the beginning to be full length. The university's Drama Division offers to do the play and it is directed by my wife.*

By the time the play is mounted, much of the conspicuous self-indulgence is gone and the play, about a fifty year old English professor on trial in his mind for real and imagined crimes, is roundly well received by students, faculty, and admin-

25

istration. (Actually I am a bit put off that the play generates no trouble.) The playwright plays the amalgam character based on his accusers. Very therapeutic.

For a number of reasons, Myles Fife is the period on a four year sentence of my life. My wife and I are divorced a month after the play runs—that act in itself a parenthetical exclamation point on the end line of a lot of infantile frailty and stupidity.

Little more than a year later, Stephanie and I walk into the Toddle House in Albuquerque. When You Comin Back, Red Ryder? is born and, in many ways, me with it.

In my fantasies about artistic success, the fruition was always pure. I had paid my dues, I deserved to enjoy it.

Forget it.

There were two moments of unadulterated purity in the *Red Ryder* experience once it left my typewriter. One was ramming my fist into the air at Seventy-second and Broadway with my first *New York Times* review tucked securely into a paper I had not read but whose content I knew beyond doubt. The second was sitting with my wife on one side of me and my agent on the other in the Blaine Thompson Advertising Agency offices above Sardi's, waiting for Clive Barnes' review of the Eastside Playhouse opening on December 5, 1973. Up and across town at the theater, Ken and the cast, those nine who had invested their hopes and gizzards in this thing too, were waiting for me to get the Barnes review and call them with the word. They didn't want to come to Sardi's again and be embarrassed. If the review was for us, they would descend like locusts. In the meantime they would continue to eat chile on the set and to keep their buttocks squeezed tightly together.

I was very drunk on Jack Daniels, which I had been drinking steadily since early afternoon when there was nothing more to do but wait. (It seemed someone's aberrant, bad joke to have to go through two Critics' Nights with the same show.) Stephanie and Gilbert were sober. Our press people and general manager whipped frantically from phone to phone, getting set to begin tallying the reviews. A T.V. review, which we would watch and which I would not remember even as I watched it, and the Barnes review would be first. Everything was in readiness. Stephanie and I sat locked hand in hand in identical silence. Gilbert hovered mother-hennishly over us, prepared to deal with the outcome. In retrospect, the idiotic vulnerability of it all is more detestable than words can tell.

Locked in my memory for all time is the picture of Leonard Mulhern, our general manager, standing in the doorway of that conference room at Blaine Thompson, holding a Xerox copy of Clive Barnes' typewritten review, saying with a simplicity that belied itself so wonderfully that I would pinch his cheek still were he here today: "Clive Barnes gave you a . . . *rave*."

I had wondered for years of course what I would do at that moment. Something *memorable*. Something they'd talk about for a long time downstairs at Sardi's: "Jesus, you think *that* was something? You shoulda seen what Medoff did when *Ryder* opened!"

The time had come to do it—whatever it was to be. So I did it: (Biographers ready?) Nothing.

I sat there.

I had nothing to say. Neither did my wife. Finally we held each other. We had come a great distance to this silence.

The moment—that pure moment—ended with word that Douglas Watt, who had come to review the play a second time, despised it a second time. The vitriol in both of his reviews prompted the side of me that won't permit the other side of me to agonize for more than twenty-four hours over any rejection to conjecture that perhaps I had once beaten him *very* badly at ping-pong in an earlier incarnation. He had been unable to forgive me. Perhaps a girl we were both crazy about witnessed the whole thing. Perhaps I had been a poor winner, rubbing his defeat in his face: "Eleven-nothing, Doug, shutout!" In the interest of fairness—a form of play really not all that interesting when one is on the defensive—let me hasten to note that I don't believe in reincarnation, so it is conceivable that the man simply despised the play and thought he was performing a public service by blasting it twice. On the other hand, perhaps the play threatened him as it does many men. On the other hand, after twenty-four hours, who, hardly, gave a damn.

I read the Barnes review to Jim Kiernan over the phone and he repeated it to the people at the theater. Within fifteen minutes we were all over each other in Sardi's. We were crazy. Delirious. We were going to be a "hit." Incredibly, wonderfully pretentious word to bandy about. We knew it! Forget about the septuagenarian Mr. Watts of the *Post*, whom we were told had napped through the play (hope the gunshot didn't startle him) and whose indecipherable piece of gibberish appeared that afternoon, and the several others, who would at least create their misgivings intelligibly, if incorrectly.

Red honey, welcome home.

The success of Red Ryder *has radically changed my life. Six of my plays have been published by Dramatists Play Service in the last year.* The Kramer *is being readied for publication by the University of Minnesota Press in its* Playwrights for Tomorrow *series. I am offered films to write; radio and television programs to be on; symposiums to sit on; pieces of paper to write my name on; people wait expectantly to hear what I have to say, as if because I can write I can also speak. Heady stuff.*

I have won the Outer Critics Circle John Gassner Award as Best Playwright for the 1973-74 season, an OBIE for Distinguished Playwrighting, and a Guggenheim Fellowship in Playwrighting. The university last spring presented me its Westhafer Award, the highest honor it has to bestow on one of its faculty and promoted me three years ahead of schedule to Associate Professor (quite a jog down the road from the Army-McCarthy hearings).

I stepped into the lead of the Chicago production of Red Ryder *on two days' notice last May, received embarrassingly good notices, and played the part for six weeks; then, while Kevin did the part in Massachusetts, I played New York for a month, reveling in playing with some of those people who have been so important to me for over a year, who played such roles in the birth of my child.*

But. Thinking about the adulterated purity of it all . . . : Friends have had difficulty dealing with what's happened to me, making me feel as if I am almost expected to apologize for making of myself what I said I would and for having achieved something they have not. A number of my colleagues at the university have displayed little fits of—as one euphemistically calls it—"healthy envy."

The gravest difficulties, though, have to do with the living of these disparate lives: one as husband and father, the other as writer—or "successful" writer, I must say, because when I was having my successes "locally," I was home most of the time or not very far away for very long. I have been gone almost half of this last year. Sometimes my wife goes with me, sometimes our daughter goes with us. None of the configurations is nearly ideal. We love Las Cruces, want to "live" here, but don't. We live several places and, if I am to continue to write for the theater, we must continue to live several places. The problem is insoluble in any simple way because the bottom line is so simple itself: If I don't write, I don't function in any other role. Two disparate lives, then, really dependent on the continuation of the one.

Simple.

When *Red Ryder* opened, General Manager Mulhern bet me it would still be running at the Eastside Playhouse on July 4, 1975. It won't be. It closed two weeks ago today after more than three hundred performances—a lot of performances by anyone's standards. But still a great disappointment. The why of it is, finally, a puzzle. When I was playing Teddy in New York, the cast assured me the reason box office had tailed off months earlier was due to bad management and that for five months management had not seemed to "care." (It must be said, though, that our management *did* keep the show running after another might have closed it.) Others blamed director and stage manager for letting the show "slip." Others credited Nixon and the economic plight of the country. Others the location of the theater (a very nice, safe neighborhood in the East Seventies but one which is not easily accessible by subway as are most of the other Off-Broadway houses, most of which are in "bad" neighborhoods). Still others felt the play had simply played its audience to depletion quite naturally. And I'm sure the puzzle has even more possible pieces. In what shape and order it should all be put together, I don't know and, in a way, don't care. It's done and I've learned what I can learn. One play, well received or not, long run or short, does not a career make.

The Eastside Playhouse will not be empty for long. *The Wager* goes into rehearsal there in four days (under different management than *Red Ryder*) and opens in four weeks. I leave wife, child, "home" once more tomorrow morning to fly to New York.

A year ago, before *Red Ryder* opened for real, I went looking for Stephen and Nancy, expecting somehow to find them in their places at the Toddle House in Albuquerque, just as Stephen and Angel are in their places each time the play is performed. I wanted to tell them what we had done to each other's lives. The Toddle House, though, was shut down and a couple of tumbleweeds stood sentinel in the overgrown front yard. I felt lonely and I started to cry and took off in a hurry.

I think of them now. I think of Fred Shaw, who died on January 2, 1971, before it all happened. I think of my son the dog, whom we gave to a family in the country who are always home. And I think of something Stephanie said to me once: You live your life, she said, as if you think you're going to die tomorrow and there's not a moment to waste.

I have no intentions of dying tomorrow. In fact, if I can keep the madmen at bay, I'm giving serious thought to living forever.

Las Cruces, N.M.
September 1, 1974

For Stephanie

When You Comin Back, Red Ryder? was first presented by the Circle Repertory Theatre Company, in New York City, in November, 1973. It was directed by Kenneth Frankel; the setting was by Bill Stabile; costumes were by Penny Davis; and the lighting by Cheryl Thacker. The cast, in order of appearance, was as follows:

STEPHEN . . . . Bradford Dourif

ANGEL . . . . Elizabeth Sturges

LYLE . . . . Addison Powell

CLARK . . . . Joe Jamrog

CLARISSE . . . . Robyn Goodman

RICHARD . . . . James Kiernan

TEDDY . . . . Kevin Conway

CHERYL . . . . Kristin Van Buren

The Circle Repertory Theatre Company production of *When You Comin Back, Red Ryder?* was subsequently moved to the Eastside Playhouse, in New York City, where it opened officially on December 6, 1973.

THE CHARACTERS

STEPHEN: *You tell 'em it was Red Ryder, everybody, drivin a Chevrolet Corvette Stingray convertible the color of money and livin in his own apartment.*

ANGEL: *I wish that if he was gonna go, that he'd just get it over with and go.*

LYLE: *Service is the name of the game.*

CLARK: *To tell ya the honest to God truth, boy, after that by-pass open, I wanted to shut down at night, but cause a your momma, I kept you on and I stayed open, to the detriment of my nearly major source of income.*

CLARISSE: *I am not your added appendage!*

RICHARD: *Edwin! It's Edwin, not Edward! Edwin Donald Snider! Now stop degrading them! We are living in the present . . .*

TEDDY: *It's no good anymore . . . It's too late.*

CHERYL: *I'm not one of them, damn it, I'm with you.*

PLACE IN TIME: A diner on the desert in southern New Mexico—six stools, three tables, a juke box. On one of the windows: FOSTER'S DINERS—ARIZ., N. MEX., TEX. The lettering has begun to chip away and although the diner is clean, its day has gone.

The rust consumes the buds and fruits of the earth;
The herds are sick; children die unborn,
And labor is vain. The God of plague and pyre
Raids like detestable lightning . . .

SOPHOCLES

Where have you gone, Joe DiMaggio
A nation turns its lonely eyes to you . . .

SIMON

ACT ONE

The jukebox plays. Morning lights come through the windows.

A boy nineteen, STEPHEN/RED, *sits at the far end of the counter reading a newspaper, his back against the partition, his feet propped on the second stool, the newspaper tabled by his thighs and knees. He is plain looking in an obtrusive way—small, his hair slicked straight back off his forehead. He wears a short sleeve sportshirt open one too many buttons at the top, the sleeves rolled several times toward his shoulders—in the last of the sixties, an unconscious parody in his dress of the mid-fifties. He smokes Raleigh cigarettes and has a tattoo, "Born Dead," on his forearm.*

The clock behind the counter reads 6:05. STEPHEN *glances irritably at it, then out the window, then at his own watch.*

STEPHEN *hears someone coming. He knows who it is. He moves to the jukebox, reaches behind it, and rejects the record that's playing. He takes his stool again and raises the newspaper so that it covers his face.* ANGEL *enters. She is perhaps several years older than* STEPHEN. *She is obese, her white uniform stretched across the rolls of her body. She has a pinched face, short hair framed by a bow made of limp, thick pastel yarn, somewhat prominent front teeth. She wears a wedding band on the ring finger of her right hand. She carries a very small purse.*

ANGEL: Good mornin, Stephen.

(STEPHEN *does not look at her, but glances at the clock and makes a strained sucking sound through his teeth—a habit he has throughout—and flips the newspaper back up to his face. Unperturbed,* ANGEL *proceeds behind the counter.*)

I'm sorry I'm late. My mom and me, our daily fight was a little off schedule today.

(STEPHEN *loudly shuffles the paper, sucks his teeth.*)

I said I'm sorry, Stephen. God. I'm only six minutes late.

STEPHEN: Only six minutes, huh? I got six minutes to just hang around this joint when my shift's up, right? This is really the kinda dump I'm gonna hang around in my spare time, ain't it?

ANGEL: Stephen, that's a paper cup you got your coffee in.
(STEPHEN is entrenched behind his newspaper.)

STEPHEN: Clark can afford it, believe me.

ANGEL: That's not the point, Stephen.

STEPHEN: Oh no? You're gonna tell me the point though, right? Hold it—lemme get a pencil.

ANGEL: The point is that if you're drinkin your coffee here, you're supposed to use a glass cup, and if it's to go, you're supposed to get charged fifteen instead of ten and ya get one of those five cent paper cups to take it with you with. That's the point, Stephen.

STEPHEN: Yeah, well I'm takin it with me, so where's the problem?

(STEPHEN has taken the last cigarette from a pack, slipped the coupon into his shirt packet and crumpled the pack. He basketball shoots it across the service area.)

ANGEL: Stephen!

(She retrieves the pack and begins her morning routine of filling salt and pepper shakers, the sugar dispensers, setting out place mats, and cleaning up the mess STEPHEN evidently leaves for her each morning. STEPHEN reaches over and underneath the counter and pulls up a half empty carton of Raleighs and slides out a fresh pack. He returns the carton and slaps the new pack down on the counter.)

What're ya gonna get with your cigarette coupons, Stephen?

(STEPHEN reads his paper, smokes, sips his coffee.)

Stephen?

(STEPHEN *lowers the newspaper.*)

STEPHEN: How many times I gotta tell ya to don't call me Stephen.

ANGEL: I don't like callin ya Red. It's stupid—callin somebody with brown hair Red.

STEPHEN: It's my name ain't it? I don't like Stephen. I like Red. When I was a kid I had red hair.

ANGEL: But ya don't now. Now ya got brown hair.

STEPHEN: (*Exasperated.*) But *then* I did and then's when counts.

ANGEL: Who says *then's* when counts?

STEPHEN: The person that's doin the *countin!* Namely yours truly! I don't call you . . . *Caroline* or . . . *Madge,* do I?

ANGEL: Because those aren't my name. My name's Angel, so—

STEPHEN: Yeah, well ya don't look like no angel to me.

ANGEL: I can't help that, Stephen. At least I was named my name at birth. Nobody asked me if I'd mind bein named Angel, but at least—

STEPHEN: You could change, it, couldn't ya?

ANGEL: What for? To what?

STEPHEN: (*Thinking a moment, setting her up.*) To Mabel.

ANGEL: How come Mabel?

STEPHEN: Yeah . . . Mabel.

ANGEL: How come? You like Mabel?

STEPHEN: I *hate* Mabel.

(STEPHEN *stares at her, sucks his teeth.*)

ANGEL: Look, Stephen, if you're in such a big hurry to get outta here, how come you're just sittin around cleanin your teeth?

STEPHEN: Hey, look, I'll be gone in a minute. I mean if it's too much to ask if I have a cigarette and a cup a coffee in peace, for chrissake, just say so. A person's supposed to unwind for two minutes a day, in case you ain't read the latest medical report. If it's too much to ask to just lemme sit here in *peace* for two minutes, then say so. I wouldn't wanna take up a stool somebody was waitin for or anything. Christ, will ya look at the waitin line to get on this stool.

ANGEL: *(Pause.)* Did you notice what's playin at the films?

STEPHEN: Buncha crap, whudduya think?

ANGEL: *(Pause.)* I saw ya circle somethin in the gift book the other mornin.

STEPHEN: What *gift* book?

ANGEL: The Raleigh *coupon* gift book.

STEPHEN: Hey—com'ere.

(Angel advances close to him. He snatches the pencil from behind her ear and draws a circle on the newspaper.)

There. Now I just drew a circle on the newspaper. That mean I'm gonna get me that car?

ANGEL: Come on, Stephen, tell me. What're ya gonna get?

STEPHEN: Christ, whudduyou care what I'm gonna get?

ANGEL: God, Stephen, I'm not the FBI or somebody. What are you so upset about? Just tell me what you're gonna get.

STEPHEN: *(Mumbling irascibly.)* Back pack.

ANGEL: What?

STEPHEN: Whudduya, got home fries in your ears?

ANGEL: Just that I didn't hear what you said is all.

STEPHEN: *Back. Pack.*

ANGEL: Who's gettin a back pack?

STEPHEN: The guy down the enda the counter. Chingado the Chicano. He's hitchin to Guatemala.

ANGEL: You're gettin a back pack? How come?

38

STEPHEN: Whuddo people usually get a back pack for?

ANGEL: Ya gonna go campin?

STEPHEN: No I ain't gonna go *camp*in. I'm gonna go gettin the hell outta this lousy little town, that's where I'm gonna go *camp*in.

ANGEL: When? I mean . . . when?

STEPHEN: When? Just as soon as I get somethin taken care of.

ANGEL: When will that be?

STEPHEN: When will that be? When I get it taken care of— when d'ya think. Lemme have a donut .

ANGEL: *(Getting him a donut.)* Where ya gonna go?

STEPHEN: Where am I gonna go? I'm gonna go hitchin that way *(Pointing left.)* or I'm gonna go hitchin that way *(Pointing right.)* and when I get to some place that don't still smella Turdville here I'm gonna get me a decent job and I'm gonna make me some bread.

(He picks up the donut and bites into it.)

ANGEL: Rye or whole wheat, Stephen?

STEPHEN: This is some donut. I think they glued the crumbs together with Elmer's.

ANGEL: Rye or whole wheat, Stephen?

STEPHEN: *(With his mouth full.)* Believe me, that ain't funny.

ANGEL: Don't talk with your mouth full.

STEPHEN: Christ, my coffee's cold. How d'ya like that?
(He looks at her.)

(She pours him a fresh cup of coffee in a mug. She sets it down by him. He looks at it a minute, then pours the coffee from the mug into his paper cup.)

STEPHEN: I told ya, I'm leavin in less'n two minutes.

ANGEL: That's right, I forgot.

STEPHEN: Yeah, yeah.

ANGEL: You better let your hair grow and get some different clothes if you're gonna hitch somewhere, Stephen. You're outta style. Nobody's gonna pick up a boy dressed like you with his hair like yours. And with a tattoo on his arm that says "Born Dead." People wear tattoos now that say "Love" and "Peace," Stephen, not "Born Dead."

STEPHEN: Love and peace my Aunt Fanny's butt! And who says I want *them* to pick me up, for chrissake? You think I'm dyin for a case a the clap, or what? I got a coupla hundred truck drivers come through here in the middle of the night that said they'd all gimme a ride anytime anywhere they was goin. You think I'm gonna lower myself to ride with those other morons—you're outta your mind.

ANGEL: Two hundred truck drivers? Uh-uh, I'm sorry, I have to call you on that one, Stephen. If it wasn't for Lyle's station and his motel, Lyle'd be our *only* customer.

STEPHEN: You know, right? Cause you're here all night while I'm home sacked out on my rear, so you know how many truck drivers still stop in here, now ain't that right?

ANGEL: In the three weeks since the by-pass opened, Stephen, you know exactly how many customers you had in the nights? You wanna know exactly how many, Stephen?

STEPHEN: No, Christ, I don't wanna know how many. I wanna have two minutes of peace to read my damn newspaper— if that's not askin too much! Is that askin too much? If it is, just say the word and I'll get the hell outta here and go to the goddamn cemetery or somewhere.

(LYLE STRIKER *enters. He is a man in his early sixties. He wears a brace on one leg and uses an aluminum crutch— the type with wrist and forearm supports. Beneath his hat is a proud and handsome head. In his relationship to* ANGEL *there is a sexual undertone, displaced in part to his competitiveness with* STEPHEN.)

LYLE: Mornin. Mornin.

ANGEL: Good mornin, Lyle.

LYLE: Mornin, Red.

(STEPHEN *stares blankly at* LYLE.)

(To ANGEL, *winking.)* Nice to see Red so chipper this mornin. What ya got stuck in your craw this mornin, Redbird?

(STEPHEN *sucks his teeth.* LYLE *takes what is evidently his stool.* ANGEL *sets a mug of coffee before him and begins to get his breakfast together. She glances meaningfully down at* STEPHEN.)

ANGEL: How's business, Lyle?

LYLE: All eight rooms full up last night. That's seventeen outta twenty days since the by-pass open up. Most of 'em already checked out. Looks like my new sign gonna pay off right handsomely.

STEPHEN: Damn thing's high enough. Ya oughta get yourself some collision insurance in case a couple airplanes crash into it.

LYLE: Well now, least I don't have billboards strung up and down the highway like dirty underdrawers proclaimin my whereabouts.

STEPHEN: Don't tell me about it.

LYLE: "Steak and eggs our specialty." *(Laughing.)* Steak and eggs're ever'body's specialty.

STEPHEN: Yeah, well don't tell me about it. Tell Clark.

LYLE: You tell Clark. I got enough trouble with my gas and oil people.

STEPHEN: Yeah, you got it real tough, Lyle. You lead a real tough life, I'm tellin ya.

LYLE: Well now, if you think it's so easy a life that I lead, Red, I hereby will it to ya for one day and let's see how you like takin care of an eight unit motel and a gas and service station entire by yourself.

STEPHEN: Keep sittin there babblin, Lyle, and you're gonna miss about fifty dollars wortha business from that Cadillac

41

sittin out there for the last half hour waitin for you to quit makin speeches and get off your keister and give 'em some gas.

(LYLE *turns on his stool, sees that* STEPHEN *is telling the truth.*)

LYLE: Didn't hear 'em pull up.

(LYLE *takes a swig of his coffee and hustles up.*)

STEPHEN: Came right outta room four and drove twenty feet to the premium pump. Been searchin the countryside for somebody to fill that yacht up with about fifty dollars wortha gas.

LYLE: Back shortly. Keep my seat warm. (*Winks at* ANGEL *and exits.*)

STEPHEN: (*Yelling after him:*) Yeah, gonna build a fire under it. (*Pause; to* ANGEL.) Christ, will you look at that yacht. Looks like the goddamn Queen Mary. Ya wanna bet he clears fifty bucks fillin that tank up?

ANGEL: They don't look like they oughta be stayin at Lyle's, do they?

STEPHEN: What'sa matter, the ole Cripple's ain't good enough for ya now that ya had your debutante comin out?

ANGEL: Very funny, Stephen.

STEPHEN: Ain't fancy enough for their Cadillac to sit in fronta number four of—that what you're sayin?

(STEPHEN *goes to the window to look toward* LYLE'S.)

ANGEL: Lyle's isn't exactly the Ramada Inn, ya know.

STEPHEN: Yeah? I'll take it. The Crip don't want it, let him give it to me. He ever mentions to ya he's thinkin about givin it away, you toss my name in the hat as a willin bene-fice'rary. Christ, I could really do somethin with the layout he's got.

ANGEL: Why don't ya ask Lyle to hire ya on? I bet he would.

42

What do ya wanna bet if ya asked him to hire ya on to help out at the station and the motel, he'd hire ya.

STEPHEN: *(Returning to his stool.)* I told ya, I'm hitchin outta here. And after this deal, I'm through workin for the other guy. The next job I get, it's gonna be workin for Number One here.

ANGEL: Oh yeah? What're gonna do?

STEPHEN: Don't you worry about me. Okay?

ANGEL: Yeah, but what're ya gonna *do*, Stephen?

STEPHEN: What am I gonna do? I'm gonna come drivin up to your door one day in a Chevrolet Corvette Stingray convertible the color of money is what I'm gonna do. Then I'm gonna rev up that four-ten engine through my glasspack mufflers and I'm gonna lay about four hundred feet a rubber down your street.

(Pause. He looks from a distance to her.)

Anybody pull a stunt like that on your street one day, you be sure and tell 'em who it was. You tell 'em it was Red Ryder, everybody, drivin a Chevrolet Corvette Stingray convertible the color of money and livin in his own apartment. You be sure and tell 'em.

ANGEL: I'll tell them, Stephen.

STEPHEN: You tell 'em it was Red Ryder and from now on he's workin for Number One.

ANGEL: What kinda work's Number One gonna be *doin* though, Stephen?—

STEPHEN: And I'll tell ya one thing. When I'm ready to go, I'm gonna write a letter to the goddamn *company* tellin 'em what the hell kinda deal I think Clark's givin us out here.

ANGEL: Hey, do me a favor. Never mind the company. Just get Mr. Clark in here when I'm around and tell him off. I'd pay money to see that.

STEPHEN: I ain't gonna waste my time talkin to Clark. He's

just runnin a lousy franchise. When I quit, I'm writin a
registered letter to the company. I'm writin a registered
letter to ole man Foster hisself.

ANGEL: I'd pay twenty bucks to see ya read off Mr. Clark.

STEPHEN: You ain't got twenty bucks.

ANGEL: *(Sticking out her hand.)* You wouldn't care to bet on
that, would ya?

STEPHEN: How much money you got?

*(ANGEL sticks her tongue into her cheek and takes a crack
at a haughty look.)*

You probably got three, four thousand stored up. Ya never
do a damn thing but come to work, watch television with
that ole Cripple out there, and go home to get ready to do
the same goddamn thing all over again.

*(He snaps the newspaper up. His remark is true enough to
hurt her visibly.)*

(Pause.)

ANGEL: How long you been workin here, Stephen?

STEPHEN: I don't keep tracka time.

ANGEL: You know how long I been workin here?

(STEPHEN reads his paper.)

Fourteen months. Ya know how many times I asked Mr.
Clark for a raise?

(STEPHEN sucks his teeth, reads his paper.)

STEPHEN: Your problem is ya shouldn't ask *him* nothin.

ANGEL: He's the *boss*, Stephen—

STEPHEN: What ya should do is write a registered letter direct
to the company.

ANGEL: What should I tell them?

STEPHEN: Christ, tell em you're out here in goddamn New
Mexico gettin the royal shaft from Clark and that either

they make him cough up that raise or they can do you know what with their lousy job.

ANGEL: I think you're right, Stephen.

STEPHEN: I *know* I'm right.

ANGEL: You should have a raise too. If they think workin the graveyard shift is easy, let 'em try it sometime. Who'd Mr. Clark get if you quit?

STEPHEN: Who? No one, that's who. Ole Clark'd have to work hisself. (*Laughs.*) That'd do my heart good, to see ole Clark in here at three a.m. hashin potatoes. I think maybe I'll threaten to quit unless he gives me a raise and see what he says to that.

ANGEL: I'll bet he'll give ya one pretty darn quick, that's what I bet. You should do it, Stephen.

STEPHEN: I just might do it today.

(TOMMY CLARK *enters in a big hurry, carrying two plastic bags full of red chile pods.*)

ANGEL: Good mornin, Mr. Clark.

CLARK: Here's the chile for the enchilada lunch special. Get right on 'em.

(CLARK *zips into the kitchen area.*)

ANGEL: (*To* STEPHEN.) Do it, Stephen.

(CLARK *dumps the chile, opens the cash register, glances at the drawer, whips it shut, and turns on* STEPHEN.)

CLARK: That's a five cent cup ya got your coffee in, Red.

STEPHEN: I was just leavin.

CLARK: Nickels don't grow on trees, boy—leastwise not on one a the ones in the Clark yard.

STEPHEN: Yeah, well—

CLARK: (*To* ANGEL.) Back in about an hour to check the books.
(STEPHEN *has returned to his stool and propped his feet up on the next stool.*)

45

Double cut that chile with water. Couldn't get the milder ones. (*To* STEPHEN.) Yore momma let ya stick your feet on her furniture at home, Red?

(STEPHEN *snaps his feet from the stool.*)

(*To* ANGEL.) Let's get the Sunday Special sign up. Chop, chop. Be lunch before ya know it.

(CLARK *glances at* STEPHEN *and exits in a hurry.*)

Back shortly.

(*Silence.* ANGEL *cannot look immediately at* STEPHEN. *Combating his humiliation,* STEPHEN *slaps his feet back up on the adjacent stool.* ANGEL *takes a toothpick from the dispenser and chews on it. After a moment she glances at the clock.*)

ANGEL: Boy, Mr. Clark was sure in a good mood this mornin, wasn't he? (*Pause.*) Isn't your guardian gonna pick ya up this mornin?

STEPHEN: My . . . *what?*

ANGEL: I don't know. What do you call him? Your stepfather. That's right, you call him your stepfather.

STEPHEN: I call him Ray. I don't call him my stepfather. I call him Ray. Who calls anybody "your *step*father"?

ANGEL: (*Putting up the Sunday Special enchilada sign.*) Well, isn't *Ray* gonna pick ya up?

STEPHEN: Lemme have one a them toothpicks.

ANGEL: (*Getting the toothpick.*) Who's pickin ya up?

STEPHEN: *No*body's pickin me up. Somebody gotta pick me up before you're happy?

ANGEL: He just always picks ya up on a Sunday.

STEPHEN: Two Sundays!

ANGEL: Seems like more'n two.

STEPHEN: Two.

ANGEL: (*Pause.*) He's not pickin ya up?

46

STEPHEN: *No*, he ain't pickin me *up*.

ANGEL: *(Pause.)* Your mom pickin ya up?

STEPHEN: *No*body's pickin me up. My mom don't got a car in the first place.

ANGEL: She's got Ray's car.

STEPHEN: Ray's on vacation.

ANGEL: Where'd they go?

STEPHEN: Ray. Ray. Not they. Ray. Ray went on vacation last Wednesday.

ANGEL: By *himself*?

STEPHEN: *(Mimicking her.)* Yeah, by *hi*sself.

ANGEL: What do you call that?

STEPHEN: I don't call it nothin. Ya gotta attach a label to it, call it what they call it.

ANGEL: Well, what do they call it?

STEPHEN: They call it a legal separation. I call it a royal screwin of my ole lady. He left her with maybe five bucks to her name and the lousy house that was hers to start with. That's some profiit for eighteen months hard labor.

ANGEL: *(Pause, trying to lighten the load.)* Well, ya could always look at it that people aren't supposed to get paid for hard labor.

STEPHEN: You think that's funny? I'll tell ya a secret: That ain't funny.

ANGEL: *(Pause.)* Sometimes I think my mom and me oughta get a legal separation.

STEPHEN: Yeah, then you and the Crip could set up Home Sweet Home inside his color television.

ANGEL: Oh Stephen.

STEPHEN: Christ, look what's comin. Put on your ballerina formal, we're gonna have a concert.

(ANGEL *moves down toward* STEPHEN's *stool to get a look out.* CLARISSE *(pronounced Clar-*EESE*) and* RICHARD ETHREDGE *enter. They are an attractive, informally well-dressed couple in their late thirties, early forties.* RICHARD *is as sure of himself as* CLARISSE *is reserved.* RICHARD *takes a deep whiff of the air in the diner as he steps decisively through the door.* CLARISSE *has preceded him uneasily; she carries a violin case.* ANGEL *and* STEPHEN's *attention is drawn from the* ETHREDGES *to the violin case.)*

RICHARD: *(To* ANGEL.*)* Hi.

(STEPHEN *flips up his newspaper before he has to find out whether the man will say hello to him also.)*

ANGEL: Good mornin.

(CLARISSE *moves toward the far booth.)*

RICHARD: Ah-ah—got to sit at the counter.

CLARISSE: Richard, I'd rather—

(RICHARD *shakes his head, smiles, and points expansively to the counter. They sit in the middle of the line of stools.* CLARISSE *places the violin on the counter with mechanical care.)*

RICHARD: What did I tell you? Just smell that.

ANGEL: Have you eaten here before or somethin?

RICHARD: Oh no. I grew up in New York. Spent a lot of my mis-spent youth hanging around diners.

ANGEL: What'll it be? Steak and eggs is our specialty.

RICHARD: *(To* CLARISSE.*)* Hon . . . ?

CLARISSE: Just coffee and a danish.

RICHARD: My wife would like a cup of black coffee, please, and a sweet roll toasted and buttered.

ANGEL: Uh-oh. *(Indicating the small collection of sweet rolls and donuts.)* These are from yesterday still. They're pretty stale. Sweet roll man doesn't come on a Sunday. How bout steak and eggs. That's our specialty anyway.

48

(RICHARD *looks to* CLARISSE.)

CLARISSE: Do you have a half a grapefruit?

ANGEL: Sure!

CLARISSE: I'll have that, and an egg and a piece of toast.

RICHARD: All right, I think we're on our way. The grapefruit, one egg scrambled dry, a piece of toast on the light side, and coffee, black.

ANGEL: How bout you? Like to try the steak and eggs?

RICHARD: No, I don't believe so. Let me have two eggs scrambled dry, a couple of pieces of toast—closer to toasted than my wife's—a glass of orange juice, and coffee.

ANGEL: Comin up. (*She turns to her work.*)

RICHARD: Is there someplace I can pick up a Sunday paper?

ANGEL: Pass the paper, Stephen.

(STEPHEN *ignores her.*)

RICHARD: Oh no, I don't want to take his paper.

ANGEL: *Steph*en.

RICHARD: Isn't there a machine or—

ANGEL: (*Moving toward* STEPHEN.) This is the customer paper. He works here. (*As a joke and afterthought, taking the paper from* STEPHEN.) He can't read anyway. He just looks at the pictures.

(*The* ETHREDGES *smile politely.* LYLE *enters.*)

LYLE: All set for ya. Came to eight seventy-five.

(LYLE *feeds* RICHARD *a dollar bill and a quarter change.*)

RICHARD: Ah—fine. Thanks very much.

LYLE: No trouble. Key's in the ignition. (*To* ANGEL.) All right, kiddo, bring on my breakfast.

(STEPHEN *goes behind the counter for some more coffee. His attitude intends to suggest to the* ETHREDGES *that he can go behind the counter and they can't.*)

STEPHEN: Christ, I gotta get outta here.

ANGEL: You oughta go home and get some sleep, Stephen.

STEPHEN: I ain't talkin about sleep. I'm talkin about gettin *outta* here.

LYLE: Made up your mind where ya wanna go, Red?

STEPHEN: How bout anywhere's more'n ten miles away from this hog trough.

ANGEL: How bout as far away as next door?

STEPHEN: Aw, shut up!

LYLE: Hey now, Redbird, that's no way to talk to a lady.

STEPHEN: *(Elaborately looking around.)* Lady? I don't see no lady. *(Lighting on* CLARISSE.*)* Pardon me, m'am, I did not see ya sittin there.

LYLE: What is it that you're insinuatin in my direction, Angel?

ANGEL: Stephen'll kill me.

LYLE: Stephen will not kill ya. Speak up.

ANGEL: I was just tellin Stephen that if he was sick of workin here that why didn't he ask you if ya could hire him on to help ya out with the station and the motel.

LYLE: Uh-huh. Tha's very int'restin, indeed.

ANGEL: Could ya do that, Lyle?

LYLE: Oh yes—uh-huh, could do that.

ANGEL: Ya could?

*(*ANGEL *looks to* STEPHEN, *who picks and sucks his teeth, ignores them.)*

LYLE: I don't suppose that the Redhead has informed ya that not once but three times I have offered him in the last two months to come to work for me in the very capacity to which you allude.

STEPHEN: I'm gettin *outta* here. How many times I gotta tell you guys that before it sinks into your thick skulls.

LYLE: Where are ya *goin* though, son?

STEPHEN: If it's any of your lousy business, a girl that I went to high school with's ole lady that moved to Baton Rouge said when they were in for a visit at Christmas that if I was ever leavin here and wanted to go to work for her that I should come on over to Baton Rouge and they'd put me to work in a *decent* job.

ANGEL: What girl's mom?

STEPHEN: Kay Williams'!

ANGEL: *(Pause.)* She owns a restaurant, Stephen.

(LYLE laughs caustically.)

STEPHEN: Nooooo . . .

ANGEL: What'd be the difference? I mean, what'd—

STEPHEN: *(Laughing sarcastically.)* The difference'd be that this is a lousy hog trough and that's a *res*taurant—that's what'd be the difference. Ya wear a tuxedo there, for chrissake! The waitresses wear long skirts and ruffle blouses, not nurses' uniforms. And ya carry *food* out on a *tray*, ya don't sling hash across a grimy formica airstrip.

LYLE: Well why don't ya go on and *go*? What's holdin ya back?

STEPHEN: If it's any of your lousy business, Lyle, I got somethin I gotta take care of first.

LYLE: Uh-huh, and what's that?—

STEPHEN: And I'll tell ya, when I got that somethin taken care of, you ain't gonna have to build no fire under my butt to get me outta here.

LYLE: What is it that ya have to take care of?

STEPHEN: No offense, Lyle, but that's none of your lousy business.

LYLE: If it's buyin your momma that automobile . . . *(Pause.)* Prez Potter and me go back a lotta way, son. He mentioned you was in to his lot the other afternoon.

51

(STEPHEN *storms out of the diner.* LYLE *smiles with a certain pride of accomplishment and glances fleetingly at* ANGEL.)

ANGEL: *(To* RICHARD.*)* I hope ya don't get indigestion from Stephen.

RICHARD: Oh no. Don't worry about it.

ANGEL: If ya wanna file a complaint or anything, I have forms Mr. Clark left—

RICHARD: No no, don't be silly.

ANGEL: Stephen don't mean nothin by all the noise he makes. He just needs to make a lotta noise.

LYLE: I just wish he'd put up or shut up. That's all I ask of him. A person oughta put up or shut up.

ANGEL: I wish that if he was gonna go, that he'd just get it over with and go.

(STEPHEN *returns with a fresh newspaper.*)

STEPHEN: Hey, Lyle, coupla weirdoes just pushed a VW van into the station. Look like just your type.

LYLE: If you was there, why didn't ya help 'em? You know how to pump gas.

STEPHEN: Like I said, they ain't my type.

(LYLE *starts to get up.*)

Aw, sit there and eat your slop. They're comin in here. Yessireebob, they sure ain't *my* type. They might be yours but they sure ain't mine.

(STEPHEN *snort-laughs, flips up his paper.*)

(TEDDY *and* CHERYL *enter.* TEDDY *is 30-35, wears an army fatigue jacket and has long hair.* CHERYL *is no more than 20. She wears jeans, a tank top and a light shawl. She is pretty in a straight-haired, unwashed, no makeup way. She is bra-less; this fact generates helpless interest in* STEPHEN, *an interest which he tries all too obviously to hide.* LYLE, *too, is drawn to her breasts, though less obviously and less frequently than* STEPHEN.*)

(TEDDY *stops inside the door and looks across the diner. He owns the room; he is made of mercury.*)

ANGEL: Good mornin.

(TEDDY *is silent a long moment. He turns to smile at* CHERYL.)

TEDDY: (*Affecting a stereotyped southwestern accent.*) Mornin, neighbors.

(TEDDY *starts upstage, between the counter and the booth inside the door. When he is abreast of* CLARISSE, *he suddenly stops and turns to her.*)

Pardon me, m'am, but aren't you...

(CLARISSE *looks up at him. She obviously does not know him.* TEDDY *holds fleetingly on her and then averts his gaze* ...)

'Scuse me.

(... *as if he's trying to suggest that he* doesn't *recognize her when in fact he really wants to suggest that he* does. CLARISSE *and* RICHARD *exchange bewildered glances, and a strange dormant seed is planted in* RICHARD's *mind.*)

Well now ... who runs that yere fillin station next door?

(TEDDY *glances at* CLARISSE, *who is looking at him. She averts her eyes.*)

LYLE: Right here. Lyle Striker, owner proprietor and janitor.

TEDDY: Well, sir, need a rebuilt generator for a VW van.

LYLE: Nothin open today. Sunday.

TEDDY: Sunday, is it?

LYLE: Ever'body sleepin it off or out prayin forgiveness for it.

TEDDY: Tell ya what I had in mind. Thought maybe in a town such as yours a man with a service station, and a good natured crippled man to boot, would be in a position to call up a parts store on a Sunday mornin and get a part anyhow.

53

LYLE: *(Pause.)* S'pose I could.

TEDDY: We surely would appreciate it.

LYLE: Let's have a look at your van first and make sure—

TEDDY: *(Accentless.)* Don't have to look at the van.

LYLE: Wouldn't want ya to spend—

TEDDY: *(Accentless.)* Generator's gone, sir. If you'll be kind enough to get us a rebuilt, I'll install it myself.

LYLE: Well, that sounds like a tough offer to beat. *(He meets TEDDY's eyes and then has to avert his gaze.)* I'll just go on over to the station and see who I can rouse up.

TEDDY: Mighty accommodatin of ya.

LYLE: *(Rising.)* Back in a jiffy, Angel. Don't auction off my eggs now.

(LYLE winks at ANGEL, then turns and exits with a glance at CHERYL's bosom and a small follow-up smile at her face.)

ANGEL: *(As LYLE exits.)* What do I hear for Mr. Lyle Striker's eggs?

(TEDDY and CHERYL sit at the booth inside the door. CHERYL is noticeably nervous and has been since they entered.)

TEDDY: How are y'all this mornin?

ANGEL: Just fine. How're you folks?

TEDDY: Just fine. How you?

ANGEL: Fine.

TEDDY: That's fine. *(Slapping dust from his pants.)* Y'all seem to have the dust market pretty well cornered out here. *(Looking to STEPHEN, who is staring at him.)* How you, kid?

STEPHEN: I'm okay, *dad.*

TEDDY: Gladda hear it. *(To himself.)* Boy's got a sense of humor, gonna think about puttin him on T.V. *(To the ETHREDGES.)* And how bout you nice lookin folks. How you this mornin?

54

RICHARD: Excellent, thanks.

TEDDY: Excellent! *(To* CHERYL.*)* Ever'body here's fine or okay or excellent. Whudduya thinka that?

CHERYL: *(Quickly, quietly.)* Stop it.

TEDDY: The call has gone out for me to "stop it." All y'all in favor, kindly signify by raisin your hands.

CHERYL: *(To* ANGEL.*)* Do you have some coffee?

TEDDY: *(To himself.)* Looks like it's gonna be a close vote.

ANGEL: *(To* CHERYL.*)* To go or to drink here?

CHERYL: Jesus—to drink here. Where are we gonna go?

ANGEL: Two?

CHERYL: *(To* TEDDY *who stares at* STEPHEN *who stares right back.)* Will you cut it out! Do you want coffee?

TEDDY: *(Turning away from* STEPHEN.*)* Yeah.

CHERYL: Two.

ANGEL: Where you folks from?

TEDDY: Istanbul. *(Pauses, then sings the rest.)* Used to be Constantinople—

STEPHEN: You got California plates.

TEDDY: *(Squinting at* STEPHEN, *gaming.)* Just who are you, mister?

(STEPHEN *sucks his teeth.)*

ANGEL: Where ya headed?

TEDDY: *Mexico.*

ANGEL: Oh, that's nice down there.

TEDDY: Get around a lot, do ya?

STEPHEN: Shee! She never been outta the state a New Mexico. She don't know.

ANGEL: I know more'n you think, Stephen. I see books and I meet a lotta nice people've been there.

55

STEPHEN: Sure ya do.

ANGEL: (*Staring at* STEPHEN, *then turning to* TEDDY *and* CHERYL.) You folks wanna order somethin to eat?

TEDDY: Don't mind if we do.

ANGEL: Steak and eggs is our specialty.

TEDDY: Steak and eggs it is then. And home fries ya sliced up with your own little fingers?

ANGEL: Stephen's fingers.

TEDDY: Well, hell, I'll take a chance.

ANGEL: M'am?

CHERYL: Yeah—fine.

TEDDY: Now, over easy on them eggs, darlin, med-jum on that beef.

ANGEL: How bout you, m'am?

CHERYL: Any way—it doesn't matter.

TEDDY: You surprise her, darlin.

(ANGEL *retreats to her grill.*)

Where you nice looking folks from San Diego in that Cadillac car headin?

RICHARD: Do you know us? You know, I got the feeling when you came in—

TEDDY: (*Winking, whispering.*) Saw the San Diego State Faculty sticker on the bumper.

RICHARD: Oh—that's my wife's.

TEDDY: Uh-huh. Thought for a second there she was my cousin Faye.

(TEDDY *and* CLARISSE *stare at each other a moment.*)

Headin back to San Diego, are ya?

RICHARD: New Orleans.

TEDDY: New Orleans. (*Nodding at the violin case.*) Packin a submachine gun?

56

RICHARD: Only a violin, I'm afraid.

TEDDY: Prefer a submachine gun, would ya?

RICHARD: *(Laughing.)* I didn't mean I was literally afraid—

TEDDY: Yes, m'am, I don't mind sayin that you tend to remind me a whole helluva lot of my cousin Fern.

(Again, TEDDY *and* CLARISSE's *eyes hold a moment.)*

That must be a mighty fine fiddle to get took to breakfast with ya.

RICHARD: It's a Guarnerius. *(Smiling.)* Sometimes I think my wife has an added appendage.

TEDDY: Lady playin the hoe-down circuit, is she?

CLARISSE: No, I'm—

*(*RICHARD *stops her from answering by touching her shoulder.)*

RICHARD: She's going to be with the New Orleans Philharmonic this summer.

TEDDY: Uncle Clyde Bob and Aunt Cissy must be mighty proud of you, Cousin Freda. *(To* RICHARD.) And you just goin along to answer the tough questions for her? Just livin off the little woman's residuals, as it were?

RICHARD: Not quite.

TEDDY: Not quite. Doctor, lawyer, or Indian chief?

*(*RICHARD *smiles indulgently.)*

Don't mean to be nosey.

RICHARD: No?

TEDDY: Just curious. Just makin a little roadside diner conversation. Pass the time. Hope ya don't mind.

RICHARD: As of yet I don't.

TEDDY: But at some future date you might. . . . Gonna jot that down here.

RICHARD: That accent you're affecting seems a form of condescension aimed at all of us.

TEDDY: Surely not. No law against havin fun, is there? Leastways, not yet.

(TEDDY *smiles broadly at* RICHARD *who smiles coolly back and goes on with his breakfast.*)

RICHARD: No. Not yet.

TEDDY: May I ask, sir, what *do* you do?

RICHARD: I am in the *im*port business.

TEDDY: *Im*port. Well well. And just what do you im*port?*

RICHARD: *Tex*tiles.

TEDDY: *Tex*tiles. Had you figured for an osteopath. (*To himself.*) Never have been able to figure what folks got against osteopaths. (*To* CHERYL.) Doctor here imports *tex*tiles.

(CHERYL *nods uncomfortably.*)

(*To himself.*) Got me on a called third strike on that one, all right. Thought it was a fast ball comin at my head and then she suddenly dives down across the plate and I'm left alookin. Live and learn. (*Turns to* STEPHEN.) And how bout my little buddy in the corner there? My, my, but I like your hair style. I'll bet that look'll be back before ya know it. Girls'll be climbin all over ya. Rolled up sleeves, the works. What do you do, buddy?

(STEPHEN *stares at* TEDDY.)

ANGEL: (*When* STEPHEN *does not answer.*) He works the graveyard shift here.

TEDDY: The graveyard shift. That must be a mighty important position. Eh, buddy?

STEPHEN: Stinks.

TEDDY: (*Putting a hand to his ear.*) Didn't quite catch that.

ANGEL: (*When* STEPHEN *doesn't repeat himself.*) He said it stinks—workin the graveyard shift.

58

TEDDY: You his agent, honey? What's the boy's long suit?

ANGEL: What do ya mean?

TEDDY: Well, I mean what's the boy *do* that's so im-pressive than an agent of your reputation took him on as a client?

ANGEL: I don't know. What's your long suit, Stephen?

(STEPHEN *stares at her with fire in his eyes.*)

TEDDY: Lad doesn't talk much, does he?

ANGEL: You should hear him when no one's around.

TEDDY: When no one's around or just when someone like me's not around?

(*Pause.*)

(*To himself.*) Like to listen in one of these days on a con-versation between my little buddy here and my cousin with the fiddle.

CLARISSE: I wasn't aware I was under any obligation to carry on a conversation.

(LYLE *enters.*)

LYLE: Well I don't mind confessin that our parts store fella wasn't tickled pink, but he'll have it up here inside fifteen minutes.

TEDDY: Obliged. Yessir, deeply o-bliged.

LYLE: Service is the name of the game.

TEDDY: I can believe it.

LYLE: Product lists at thirty-seven fifty, but he was in such an almighty hurry to get himself out on the lake before all the fish is gone, that I jewed him down to thirty-five.

TEDDY: Doggone if that ain't a bargain.

LYLE: Well I always say two and a half dollar is two and a half dollar.

TEDDY: I'll tell ya the truth, neighbor: I hope ya don't say it too often, you'd like to bore folks right outta their minds.

LYLE: (*Laughing.*) Wouldn't be a bit surprised.

TEDDY: (*Laughing.*) No sir, I wouldn't either. (*He stops laughing.*) I surely wouldn't.

(LYLE *stops laughing. Then* TEDDY *lets out one more burst.* LYLE *laughs.* TEDDY *stops.* LYLE *stops, returns uncertainly to his stool.* ANGEL *has served the* ETHREDGES *during the exchange between* TEDDY *and* LYLE. *She goes after* LYLE's *breakfast.*)

RICHARD: It looks very good.

ANGEL: What? Oh—thank you.

RICHARD: Puts me right back in high school.

(LYLE *takes a bite of his breakfast.*)

LYLE: How much ya short for the car, Redbird?

(STEPHEN *ignores him.*)

Prez tells me ya got forty-five, but ya need another thirty.

STEPHEN: Prez is sure got hisself a big yap for a little ole wart of a guy, don't he?

LYLE: You wanna get outta here so bad, Red, you wanna go to Baton Rouge and wear a tuxedo, I'll lend ya the thirty dollar and you get your momma that automobile and get yourself outta here.

STEPHEN: (*Snorting.*) Yeah, sure. At what kinda interest?

LYLE: No interest, son. Just a man-to-man loan. You just send me back the money when ya can.

STEPHEN: I like payin my own way. I don't like borrowin from nobody.

LYLE: Just pay me back when ya can. Ya forget for a year or so, what the heck. Next time ya remember, ya got the money, send it on back to me.

STEPHEN: I'll hang around a while longer, if ya don't mind, and loan it to myself.

LYLE: Up to you.

STEPHEN: That's just the way I see it too.

LYLE: Welp, I'll head on back to the station and wait for that generator.

(He gobbles a last bite and gets up to leave.)

TEDDY: Much obliged. Say—how'd it come, neighbor, your infirmity there? Infantile paralysis as a child?

LYLE: Stroke.

TEDDY: **Ah.**

LYLE: Had a mild stroke back in forty-five.

TEDDY: Forty-five!—quite a year.

LYLE: Just after breakfast it was.

(LYLE heads for the door.)

TEDDY: *(Pause.)* Helluva way to start the day.

(LYLE stops, turns back to TEDDY, smiling. TEDDY stares at him.)

LYLE: I better get movin here. *(He nods and exits.)*

TEDDY: Nice old cripple, ain't he? *(To STEPHEN.)* So you wanna get outta here, do ya, little buddy? Why don't ya come on down to Mexico with us.

STEPHEN: No thanks.

TEDDY: *(Referring to STEPHEN's pointed, lace up, rather high heeled shoes.)* Ya got the shoes for it.

(STEPHEN sucks his teeth.)

(Quietly, but making no effort to close out the others.) The ole man seems pretty anxious for you to leave town. Ya notice that, boy? I did. I noticed that. Whudduyou make a that?

(STEPHEN heads for the coffee.)

Hey!—

(STEPHEN is brought up short, the others startled.)

—you got a pass to go behind that counter?

61

(STEPHEN *refills his paper cup.* TEDDY *moves to* STEPHEN's *stool and sits on it.*)

The ole man called you Red, didn't he? Now that's curious. Why would somebody call somebody else Red if that somebody else had brown hair? That short for red neck, or what?

ANGEL: He had red hair when he was a child back in Pittsburgh ... *(Pause.)* ... Pennsylvania.

TEDDY: Ah—the one in Pennsylvania, I see. But you call him Stephen.

ANGEL: I don't like to call him Red. I think it's silly to call someone with brown hair Red.

STEPHEN: Shut up, will ya!

TEDDY: Hey now, boy, don't talk thataway. I purely agree with our corpulent friend here, the agent. That is pretty silly, isn't it?

ANGEL: Not if he likes it though, I guess. I just call him Stephen.

TEDDY: Uh-huh.

ANGEL: His last name's Ryder.

STEPHEN: I told you to shut up!

TEDDY: And I told you . . .*(Exploding a laugh as the name catches up with him.)* Red Ryder! Goddamn!

ANGEL: It's all right. We know each other.

TEDDY: *(To* RICHARD.*)* You remember Red Ryder, Doc?

RICHARD: Yes. Very well.

TEDDY: Boy, I do too. There was one straight shooter. Didn't dress like a fag and sing like Roy and Hoppy. And that Little Beaver—I tell you, there was a little redskin could handle a bow and arrow. What in the hell happened to those people, doc?

RICHARD: *(Off-hand.)* Gone.

TEDDY: Gone, sir, or displaced?

(Pause.)

I'll tell ya one thing for sure, Red—those boys had guts. You got guts, Red? How would you rate your own self on a *gut* scale?

(STEPHEN sucks his teeth. Suddenly TEDDY crashes his hand down on the counter. Everyone starts. TEDDY moves toward STEPHEN gunslinger fashion.)

There ain't room enough in this yere town for you and me, Red Ryder.

(Pause.)

So I'm leavin.

(TEDDY laughs robustly at himself.)

Just as soon as I get my hoss a new generator.

(Pause.)

You're a real chickenshit, ain't ya, boy?

STEPHEN: Takes one to know one.

(TEDDY laughs happily; he spots STEPHEN's tattoo.)

TEDDY: What in the hell is that?

STEPHEN: *What?*

TEDDY: You got a tattoo on your arm that says "Born Dead."

STEPHEN: Noooo.

TEDDY: Yeah. Look. Boy, you're a walkin metaphor, ain't ya? You know what a metaphor is? *(Nothing from STEPHEN.)* *Huh?*

STEPHEN: *(Pause.)* Yeah.

TEDDY: Hogshit. What's a metaphor, boy?

STEPHEN: Well if you don't know, I'm sure as hell not gonna tell ya.

(TEDDY laughs again.)

63

RICHARD: Do you mind? We're trying to finish our breakfast.

(Pause. TEDDY stares at RICHARD.)

TEDDY: Just talkin to my friend here. We'll try to keep our voices down. Sorry.

(RICHARD turns uneasily back to his breakfast.)

(To STEPHEN.) When'd you get that tattoo?

STEPHEN: *(Pause.)* You scare me.

(TEDDY moves slowly to STEPHEN, stares into his face.)

TEDDY: *(With quiet, deadly menace.)* You bet your ass I scare you. Now, when'd you get that goddamn tattoo?

(Pause.)

STEHEN: Coupla years ago.

TEDDY: Where?

STEPHEN: Carnival.

TEDDY: Why?

STEPHEN: Felt like it.

TEDDY: No. Why? What'd it mean? Why'd you pick that one?

STEPHEN: Didn't like the others.

TEDDY: Who ya with?

(TEDDY sits in a chair adjacent to STEPHEN's.)

STEPHEN: No one.

TEDDY: Who ya with?

STEPHEN: No one.

(TEDDY grabs STEPHEN's chair and jams STEPHEN up against him.)

TEDDY: Goddamn it, who were you with?

(Pause.)

STEPHEN: Davidson.

TEDDY: Big guy.

64

STEPHEN: Whudduya mean, *big* guy?

TEDDY: I mean Davidson was a big *guy*. Basketball, football player.

STEPHEN: He wasn't so big.

TEDDY: Had a girl with him. Good lookin.

STEPHEN: She was all right.

TEDDY: Yeah, I'll bet she was all right. You and Davidson and her. Her and Davidson and dot dot dot . . . *you*. Yeah. And what'd Davidson get tattooed on his arm?

STEPHEN: Nothin.

TEDDY: Bullshit. The girl's name.

STEPHEN: So big deal.

TEDDY: And then she said, "What're you gonna get, Red Ryder? 'R. R. loves L. B.' "?

ANGEL: Who's L. B.?

TEDDY: Little Beaver, darlin. And you said, No!—because you were plenty pissed; you said, I'm gettin . . . I'm gettin *that* one: "Born Dead." You should've said, I'm puttin your name on my arm too. You should've said, Goddamn it, I'm as good as Davidson any day, you just gimme the chance to show ya. And maybe . . . maybe if you'd said that to enough pretty little girls and gotten enough of their names tattooed onto your body, you'da begun to believe you *were* as good as Davidson. *(Pause.)* Even though you weren't. *(Pause.)* Never could be. Sheeit! You disappoint me, Red Ryder.

(Silence. TEDDY *stares into* STEPHEN's *face.)*

CLARISSE: Richard, I'm finished.

RICHARD: *(Rising.)* Yes. *(To* ANGEL.*)* What do I owe you?

*(*ANGEL, *in pain for* STEPHEN, *focuses slowly on* RICHARD's *bill.)*

TEDDY: *(Still staring at* STEPHEN.*)* Hey, don't let me rush y'all out.

RICHARD: We're finished.

TEDDY: *(Backing off of* STEPHEN, *rising.)* Aw, come on, have another cup of coffee. On me.

RICHARD: Some bicarbonate perhaps.

TEDDY: Darlin, you set Madame Professor and the doctor up with some more of your wonderful coffee.

(As a form of resistance, ANGEL *keeps her head to figuring* RICHARD'*s check.)*

Pour, darlin.

(She picks up the coffee. RICHARD *and* TEDDY *lock eyes.* TEDDY *lifts his eyebrows, in effect asking* RICHARD *how he wants to play this one.* RICHARD *puts his hands over their cups, smiles at* TEDDY. CLARISSE *starts for the door.)*

Say, m'am . . . lemme take a look at that Guarnerius violin before ya go.

CLARISSE: No, I'm sorry.

TEDDY: I ain't gonna hurt it. I just always wanted to have a in-person gander at one a them.

RICHARD: *(Pause.)* Then you'll behave yourself. . . ?

TEDDY: Word of honor.

*(*RICHARD *stares at* TEDDY *a moment, then averts his eyes and nods assent.* CLARISSE *is not happy with* RICHARD'*s decision. She challenges him with her eyes. Somewhat irascibly,* RICHARD *nods at her. She lays the violin case down and opens it, but does not remove the violin.* TEDDY *stares not at the violin but at her.)*

That musta cost a pretty penny.

RICHARD: I'm not through paying for it yet.

TEDDY: How much a mechanism like that cost, if ya don't mind my askin?

RICHARD: *(Pause.)* Eleven thousand dollars.

66

TEDDY: *(Smiling all too broadly and without the accent.)* You're kidding.

(RICHARD shakes his head.)

CLARISSE: *(As angrily as she can be, given her fear of TEDDY.)* Why should he be kidding?

TEDDY: Playin the fiddle must be mighty important to you, cousin.

CLARISSE: Yes. It is.

TEDDY: Why don't you play us somethin on that there eleven thousand dollar fiddle.

(RICHARD snaps up the violin and case, returns them to CLARISSE.)

(Coldly.) Why not?

CLARISSE: *(To RICHARD.)* Can we please get out of here.

RICHARD: Yes. *(To TEDDY.)* We're in a bit of a hurry. Maybe you'll catch her in concert one of these days.

TEDDY: Then again, maybe I'll catch her in something else this day.

RICHARD: I'm afraid I don't follow you.

TEDDY: I'd be afraid too, sir, indeed I would. *(To CLARISSE, quickly.)* Now why don't you make me a present of that there violin, cousin, and we'll call everything even.

(RICHARD laughs.)

All right, you're right, that ain't fair. Make it the violin and a small monthly allowance—but that's all I could accept.

RICHARD: *(To ANGEL, snapping his fingers.)* Miss—please!

TEDDY: I want that violin, cousin, and I swear to God you'd be wiser than you can imagine to give it to me.

RICHARD: You have a great deal of imagination, my friend.

TEDDY: And an incredible faculty it is, sir.

CHERYL: Teddy.

(CHERYL's eyes are to the window. TEDDY looks there.)

TEDDY: Generator. Landsakes, man's in a hurry. Looks like the Pony Express man, Red, passin the mail and hightailin it off. *(To RICHARD and CLARISSE.)* Well, it appears you ain't gonna make me a present of that there Guarnerius violin, so . . . if ya gotta go, they say, ya gotta go. You ever hear that one, Red?

(RICHARD turns to ANGEL. CLARISSE closes the violin case and moves to the door. TEDDY stares at CLARISSE who becomes uncomfortably conscious of his stare. Compulsively she snaps her eyes to his, but of course he does not look away . . . so she must. Meanwhile:)

ANGEL: That'll be two dollars and sixty cents with tax.

(RICHARD hands her three dollars.)

RICHARD: Thank you, it was very good.

(He turns and opens the door for CLARISSE.)

ANGEL: Thank *you.*

(RICHARD nods bluntly toward her, passes his eyes across TEDDY's and exits behind CLARISSE, who exits purposefully and head down, acknowledging no one.)

(Calling after them.) Come see us again.

(ANGEL lifts a hand tentatively to wave, then drops it.)

TEDDY: How's our steaks comin, darlin?

ANGEL: *(Turning quickly to the grill.)* Almost done.

TEDDY: Good. Good. He give ya a nice tip?

ANGEL: Forty cents.

TEDDY: Hot dawggy. *(Fixed out the window.)* What brought you out here from Pittsburgh, Pennsylvania, Red Ryder?

(STEPHEN says nothing.)

ANGEL: *(When STEPHEN does not answer.)* His mother had emphysema.

(TEDDY is noticeably distracted during the above and following lines, watching the ETHREDGES walk to their car.

68

CHERYL *is uneasily watching him watch them.*)

TEDDY: And the desert air cured her, did it?

(ANGEL *glances at* STEPHEN, *who stares straight ahead and smokes.*)

ANGEL: Uh-uh, she's still got it. *(Then as if she must fill space.)* You should hear her cough sometime.

TEDDY: I'm sure that'd be a real treat. Say, darlin, what's the trade like in here of a Sunday mornin? Those steaks and eggs come flyin off the griddle?

ANGEL: Uh-uh. Sunday's our worst.

TEDDY: Come on.

ANGEL: Sometimes I read the whole Sunday paper Sunday mornin.

TEDDY: Don't say.

ANGEL: Things pick up at lunchtime for the enchilada special.

TEDDY: That's nice, ain't it? Not much fun for you and the Ryder when there's no business.

ANGEL: Oh, we talk till Stephen goes home.

TEDDY: *Just* talk?

(*He turns suddenly from the window and moves from it.*)

Huh? Ya *just* talk? Tell the truth.

ANGEL: Sometimes we don't *even* talk.

TEDDY: Uh-huh.

ANGEL: Sometimes Stephen just goes home.

TEDDY: Does, does he?

ANGEL: Uh-huh.

(ANGEL *brings their food to the table, glancing intuitively toward the window.*)

TEDDY: My my, that looks *good.* *(To* CHERYL.) Dig in, honey. Just look at that grease. This where ya get the *bear* grease for your hair, Red?

ANGEL: Is it too greasy?

TEDDY: (*Ignoring her question, taking her hand.*) Com'ere darlin. Now tell the honest to God truth. When the two of you here all alone, does he ever give you a little feel?

(TEDDY *reaches up and honks one of* ANGEL'*s breasts.*)

Mee-meep!

(ANGEL *gets stuck between anger and amusement, then hustles back behind the counter.* TEDDY *looks to* STEPHEN, *who averts his eyes and storms back to his stool.* LYLE *and* RICHARD *enter.*)

LYLE: Got your generator but now these folks has lost their keys.

(LYLE *and* RICHARD *begin to look around.* ANGEL *joins in.* TEDDY *eats,* CHERYL *tries to.*)

I'll swear I left those keys in the ignition.

TEDDY: What do they look like?

RICHARD: Just a little flat piece with a ring and chain.

TEDDY: Little piece o' *tex*tile?

RICHARD: Gold.

TEDDY: My my.

LYLE: Ya know, I think I mighta left 'em on top of the premium pump.

RICHARD: (*Pause.*) Well I'll just go check on that. (*He exits.*)

LYLE: (*To* TEDDY, *when the door has closed.*) Son . . .

(TEDDY *doesn't look up.*)

I thought I'd do ya a bit of a favor . . . so I went ahead and dismounted your air coolin shroud so's I could take off your old generator.

TEDDY: Uh-huh.

LYLE: Now, son, I like to think I'm a man that understands our young folks and I'm a man that minds his own business . . .

70

TEDDY: That's a fine approach to life, sir, a fine approach.

LYLE: . . . but you could surely find yourself in a passle of trouble if one of those Mexican border guards was to get the idea to search around and find what you got taped into that shroud.

(TEDDY stares at LYLE a moment and then ducks his head back to his food. Pause.)

And I'd surely hate to see ya compound your problems by takin that man's keys.

(TEDDY glances up and holds on LYLE, forcing LYLE to avert his eyes, diverting the truth along with them.)

I ain't makin any accusations, ya understand. I'm a man that minds my own business—

TEDDY: Seems to me you said that. *(To CHERYL.)* Didn't he say that a while back?

CHERYL: *(Tensely trying to be cool.)* Yes.

TEDDY: Goddamn if I didn't think as much. Ole man, you're repeatin yo'self. *(To himself.)* 'Fraid for a second there I was goin crazy.

LYLE: Just gimme the keys if ya got 'em son. I'll say I had 'em in my pocket the whole time and didn't know it. Then I'll go out there and put that new generator on and you can be on your way.

TEDDY: Damn, ole crippled guy, if you haven't gone and complicated things. Didn't I tell you first thing that I'd put that generator in.

LYLE: I just thought I'd do ya a bit of a favor.

TEDDY: Goddamn if you didn't say that before too.

LYLE: Ya got nothin to worry about. Like I said—

TEDDY: *(Rising suddenly.)* Say it again, ole man, and I'll cut your tongue right out of your throat.

(Pause. He glances to the window.)

Now here comes Gentleman Jim and Our Lady of the Violin. How you gonna feel if they found those keys?

LYLE: I'll apologize. I surely will.

TEDDY: All right then—let's just see what develops here.

(The ETHREDGES *enter.)*

Found 'em, did ya?

RICHARD: No we didn't.

LYLE: *(Looking at* TEDDY *who looks at him; pause.)* The boy's got 'em.

*(*TEDDY *rushes* STEPHEN, *grabs him off his stool, turns him upside down and begins to shake him.* STEPHEN *struggles, but* TEDDY *is much the stronger.)*

TEDDY: All right, Red Ryder, cough up them keys. What's the Lone Ranger and Tonto gonna say when—

STEPHEN: *You got 'em, you goddamn stupid son of bitch!*

*(*TEDDY *dumps* STEPHEN, *stares at him, evidently deeply hurt.)*

TEDDY: That's a vicious thing to say, boy. You're gonna make it rough for white and Indian couples all over the country with that kinda behavior.

RICHARD: You have my keys?

TEDDY: Well . . . now this is just speculatin, ya understand, but let's speculate here a second—

RICHARD: *(Clipped.)* Do you have my keys?—

TEDDY: Just a minute—I'm speculatin, goddamn it. Let's say for the sake of speculation that I do have your keys. Now I wonder—if I did have 'em—if you'd be willing to cough up a little ransom money to get 'em back. Just in the nature of speculation of course.

LYLE: Give him the keys, son.

TEDDY: Whudduya say, Gentleman Jim?

RICHARD: If you do have my keys, I can assure you I'm not about to pay one red cent to get them back.

TEDDY: Then—just speculatin again—were I to be the po-ssessor of your keys, I just don't think I'd give 'em back. No sir, I just don't think I would. *(To himself.)* Couldn't. Impractical.

RICHARD: *(To LYLE.)* Do you have a policeman in town?

LYLE: Sheriff.

RICHARD: Would you mind calling him? We'll let him see if he can find my keys.

TEDDY: Now—just speculatin again, if you'll beg my rapidly diminishin pardon here—I wouldn't do that. No sir, I just wouldn't.

RICHARD: *(To LYLE.)* If you won't, kindly tell me the number and I will.

(RICHARD takes a step toward the phone. TEDDY rises. RICHARD stops. They face each other.)

LYLE: Son, my offer still stands.

TEDDY: And I appreciate your offer, ole man, but this here speculatin I'm doin is an offer of a different stripe.

LYLE: Then I'm gonna have to call Sheriff Garcia.

TEDDY: I pray to the very funny Lord that you don't attempt that, sir.

LYLE: Then give the man his keys back!

TEDDY: Darn it all, I can't do that.

(LYLE starts for the phone on the wall. TEDDY drops all traces of the affected accent.)

Do *not* touch that phone!

(LYLE stops.)

Now, when I say don't do something the way I just said it . . . don't do it. *(To RICHARD.)* All right, let's cut the crap, friend. We're forty-five minutes from the Mexican border and permanently out of your lives. But we've got no money to pay for our breakfast, let alone a generator. We need money.

LYLE: Have the breakfast on me, son. Put their breakfast on my tab, Angel. Have the generator on me too. Let's just don't do anything you'll be sorry for. My offer still stands. You go calmly outta here and—

TEDDY: We accept breakfast and the generator with thanks, ole man, but we've still got to have money. In the hand. And I'm damn sure that there's not enough in this register here to make cleanin it out worth my while, so if Gentleman Jim doesn't come up with, say, three hundred dollars in cash, I'm going to be very upset. What do you say, Jim?

(TEDDY *has slipped the keys from his jacket and approaches* RICHARD, *holding the keys out in his palm. Suddenly* RICHARD *leaps for the keys but* TEDDY, *anticipating, secures them in a closed fist.*)

See that move, Red Ryder? Fastest fist in the West. Can I sign on as Little Beaver with moves like that?

(RICHARD *breaks for the door.* TEDDY *leaps between* RICHARD *and the door. Like a basketball player,* RICHARD *tries to fake one way and go the other around* TEDDY, *but* TEDDY *stays between him and the door.* RICHARD *loses his balance as* TEDDY *moves at him and falls against the table with* TEDDY *and* CHERYL*'s dishes on it.*)

(*Suddenly* ANGEL *breaks for the door, but* CHERYL *leaps up and blocks the way with what is, in fact, a nearly totally ineffectual stance against* ANGEL*'s bulk should she decide to burst through.*)

CHERYL: Please don't do anything.

ANGEL: (*Screaming in* CHERYL*'s face close to tears.*) They're nice people!

TEDDY: (*To* ANGEL.) You just shift your tank in reverse and back over behind that counter—

(*During* TEDDY*'s exchange with* ANGEL, RICHARD *has stepped* *close enough to* TEDDY *to hit him. Rather than coldcocking him, however,* RICHARD *slaps him across the face.* TEDDY *drops the keys and* RICHARD *grabs them.)*

Christ, Jim, what if I'd been wearing contact lenses?

RICHARD: We're walking out of here. We're going over to Mr. Striker's station and we're getting in our car. You have as long as it takes us to locate the sheriff and get him out here to get your car fixed and be gone.

*(*RICHARD *puts an arm around* CLARISSE'S *shoulders and starts them for the door.* TEDDY *pulls a small caliber revolver.)*

TEDDY: Hold it!

(The ETHREDGES *hold it.)*

CHERYL: *Teddy!*

RICHARD: Don't you *dare* point that thing at me.

TEDDY: Empty your pockets on the table.

RICHARD: I will not.

TEDDY: Friend, I don't need to shoot you, but if that's what it's going to take to make clear who's controlling this, then that's the way it's going to have to be.

RICHARD: That's the way it's going to have to be then.

*(*TEDDY *fires the gun at* RICHARD *and, simultaneously, the stage goes black.)*

ACT TWO

Some minutes later. RICHARD *is the center of attention, seated at one of the tables, a first aid kit set out before him* LYLE *putting the finishing touches on a wrapping of gauze and two-inch tape.* CLARISSE *sits beside* RICHARD. TEDDY *is eating the last of* CHERYL's *breakfast, having finished his own. His revolver sits on the table close to him.*

TEDDY: How ya feeling, Gentleman Jim?

(RICHARD *does not respond.* TEDDY *turns to* STEPHEN *on his stool at the counter.*)

No more'n a flesh wound, Red. He'll be ready to ride by sun up. *(To* ANGEL.*)* Darlin, them's was mighty fine vittles.

LYLE: I think the bleedin's stopped.

TEDDY: Didn't I just get through tellin Red Ryder it weren't nothin more'n a flesh wound?

LYLE: *(To* RICHARD.*)* How do ya feel?

RICHARD: I'm all right.

TEDDY: *(To himself.)* Christ, I'm bein ostracized.

(LYLE *moves away from* RICHARD *and examines* CHERYL's *breasts as he rolls his sleeves back down and fastens them.*)

CLARISSE: Can I do something?

RICHARD: No, really, I'm fine. Just shaken.

CLARISSE: Please let me do something.

RICHARD: There's nothing for you to do.

TEDDY: Red, ya know who I wished coulda been here to see the looks on ever'body's faces when I put the hot lead to Jim? Cisco and Pancho. There was a couple of boys could really appreciate a good facial expression.

(TEDDY *stares at* STEPHEN, *turns angrily away, seems to get lost in himself somewhere.*)

76

Goddamn, where did all those people get to so fast? *(Pause.)* Where the hell's goddamn Tim Holt, Jim? Johnny Mack and the Durango Kid? *(Pause.)* Lash LaRue. *(Pause.)* Jesus Christ, somebody pulled a fast one.

(TEDDY *stares into the distance.*)

CHERYL: *(Agitatedly, impulsively.)* Will you stop staring at my breasts, please!

(LYLE's *and* STEPHEN's *eyes dart away.*)

TEDDY: *(Fixing on* LYLE.*)* Who's starin at your breasts, darlin?

LYLE: Not me.

TEDDY: Not you, old man?

LYLE: Not me.

TEDDY: Stuff like that don't interest you no more, do it?

LYLE: Well now, I wouldn't say that.

TEDDY: *(Utterly unamused.)* No. I wouldn't either.

(TEDDY *turns on* STEPHEN. *The menacing quality he exhibited in the first act seems suddenly colored now—and becomes more intense as the second act proceeds—by some internal wellspring set rumbling by his searching after those missing heroes.*)

STEPHEN: Who says I'm lookin at 'em?

TEDDY: I say, boy. *(Pause.)* But then she's got 'em right out there for you *to* look at, don't she? She don't want you fellas to look at her bosom, she oughta cover the thing up. Ain't that right?

(STEPHEN *barely nods.* TEDDY *stares into him.*)

CHERYL: Could we please get *out* of here?

(TEDDYS *continues to stare at* STEPHEN, *his breath coming a little bit fast.*)

Teddy . . .

TEDDY: Yeah. Why don't you and Mr. Striker go on over to the gay-rage and put our new generator in. Put the gun in your

77

shawl, sweetheart. Mr. Striker, you go on now, but I surely hope, sir, that you won't attempt nothin bay-roque. *(Handing* CHERYL *the gun.)* I'd hate for my little gal to have to decide if she'd use that thing.

LYLE: You have my word. I just want to see you out of here and us no worse off than we are now.

*(*TEDDY *snaps his eyes to* LYLE, *stares at him hard.)*

TEDDY: That's a good ole man. *(Pause.)* Goddamn but you're good, ain'cha? *(Pause.)* Yeah. You're a . . . good . . . ole . . . man. Ain'cha? *(Pause.)* You keep your eyes off my little gal's breasts. You understand me?

*(*LYLE *lifts his chin, stares ahead.)*

(To CHERYL.*)* Bring back a coupla rolls of friction tape.

CHERYL: *(Quietly.)* Teddy, I'm scared.

TEDDY: Run along, darlin.

(He crosses to her, kisses her lightly on the mouth. She touches his chest. He removes her hand and moves away from her. Pause.)

CHERYL: Go ahead, Mr. Striker. I'll follow you.

*(*LYLE *looks around, as if checking to see somehow that everyone is all right, then exits, followed by* CHERYL.*)*

TEDDY: *(To* STEPHEN.*)* Shame on you, boy. *(He stares deeply into* STEPHEN.*)* What's goin on in your mind, boy?— way back there in the corners where you never been before? Don't let it touch ya, boy, ya hear me? Ya do and it's just liable to eat you whole.

(Silence. STEPHEN *is unsure how to respond to what seems an almost intimate tone. He meets* TEDDY's *eyes a moment, then drops his eyes into* TEDDY's *fatigue jacket.* TEDDY *continues to stare at him, to stay tight to him.* STEPHEN *glances back up at* TEDDY's *eyes.)*

Go ahead, boy. Ask me somethin.

(Pause.)

STEPHEN: Were you in the war?

TEDDY: Yeah. You?

STEPHEN: Uh-uh.

TEDDY: Unfit . . . or pull a lucky number?

STEPHEN: Three-twenty-four.

TEDDY: That's too bad, ain't it? Ya mighta got yourself shot to shit and mailed home in a plastic garbage bag and buried down the road here. Ever'body woulda come to the funeral. You'da *been* somebody then, Red.

STEPHEN: Boy I went to high school with got killed in the war.

TEDDY: Uh-huh.

(Pause. STEPHEN can't remember the boy's name. He finally turns to ANGEL.)

ANGEL: Billy Simon.

STEPHEN: Billy Simon.

TEDDY: *(Smiling caustically from ANGEL to STEPHEN.)* Yeah— you'da been somebody, Red. I knew a *lotta* good ole boys *became* somebody by gettin their good ole asses shot off. . . . I can't remember their names either.

(TEDDY stares at STEPHEN, then turns abruptly away.)

I wanted to go away once too, boy. Figured one place was as bad as another. *(Glancing at CLARISSE.)* Went to college. Ya know what I remember? How to do the tired swimmer's carry—which ain't much use, say, here in the desert—and the succession of Tudor-Stuart kings and queens—which ain't *no* use even if ya happen to be close to water.

(He turns back to STEPHEN.)

Yeah . . . you might as well stay here, boy. Maybe some-day they'll make ya head of the parkin lot.

(TEDDY points to his coffee mug. ANGEL brings the pot.)

ANGEL: How old is she?

TEDDY: Cheryl? Eighteen, nineteen, twenty—don't rightly know, darlin. Why? She too old for me, ya think?

ANGEL: Where'd ya meet each other?

TEDDY: Sock hop. Yes'm, we bopped our little be-hinds off that first glorious night. The Kalin Twins. Chuck Berry. . . . How come they call you Angel, dumplin?

ANGEL: My momma and daddy just named me it.

TEDDY: Angel, huh? You musta meant a lot to 'em. Then anyway. When did the bulk start to come up on ya?

ANGEL: *(Pause.)* When did I start to get fat?

TEDDY: That's right, darlin.

ANGEL: When I was little.

TEDDY: Glands, was it?

ANGEL: Uh-huh.

TEDDY: How come ya wear that weddin ring on your right hand? You married to Mrs. Christ's boy?

ANGEL: My daddy gave it to me.

TEDDY: How is your daddy these days?

ANGEL: *(Pause.)* I don't know. He went away a long time ago.

TEDDY: Cause a you?

ANGEL: *(Pause.)* Cause of my momma and my gra'ma, I think.

TEDDY: You think anybody's ever gonna marry you, Angel?

ANGEL: *(Pause.)* I don't know.

TEDDY: *(Pause; without malice.)* No. Nobody ever is.

RICHARD: What the hell's the *matter* with you, man?

TEDDY: Generally, Jim, or in particular?

RICHARD: What's the matter with *all* of you?

TEDDY: Ah! All of us. You mean us here disaffected youth of the United States of A*mur*ica?

RICHARD: *Yes!*

TEDDY: We disaffected, Jim.

RICHARD: What happened to all of that Love and Peace garbage?

TEDDY: Ah! That was another group, sir. That was these other fellas. No—us, we're not in favor of Love and Peace. *(Pause.)* How bout you, Jim? You filled with Love and Peace, are ya?

RICHARD: Not right now.

TEDDY: *(To* ANGEL.*)* How bout you, darlin? You filled with Love and Peace?

ANGEL: I think so. I mean . . . I think so.

TEDDY: Like the way ya said that twice thataway, darlin. Whudduyou love, Lamb Chop?

ANGEL: My momma . . .

TEDDY: Uh-huh.

ANGEL: . . . and my gra'ma.

TEDDY: How bout old Red Ryder here. You love ole Red, don't ya, Sweet Gut?

ANGEL: *(Pause.)* I like Stephen a lot.

TEDDY: Oh, I think ya love ole Red, that's what I think. But he don't love ya back, do he? He don't *ever* stare at your bosom, do he? Lemme intercede in your behalf, darlin, and ask the boy a coupla questions.

(ANGEL *cannot respond.*)

Now, Red, how come you don't love ole Sweet Gut here? Not good enough for ya? Sharp dresser like you. Man with all the answers. How come?

STEPHEN: None of your goddamn business.

(TEDDY *leaps at* STEPHEN *and backhands him across the head, knocking him off his stool.*)

TEDDY: *Don't you ever look at my woman's breasts again, boy, or I'll hurt you real bad!*

(*He stares furiously at* STEPHEN.)

Now you get in the middle of that room.

(STEPHEN *gets up and moves to the middle of the room, trying somehow to affect a toughness even as he complies without question.*)

My God, the unspeakable audacity of a punk like you wearing a tattoo like that. The real Red Ryder would've hung 'em up if anyone were to tell him he was associated with pigshit like that. And I'll tell you somethin else: You *never* would've found the real Ryder sittin around a dump like this starin at some tourist lady's tits. I swear to goddamn Christ I'm tempted to take those eyes out of your head and cut that tattoo out of your arm.

(*Pause.*)

Now I wanna see you ride the range. You just start ridin the range around this room till I tell you to stop.

STEPHEN: Whudduya mean, ride the range?

TEDDY: I mean like when you were a kid, you little pissant. Ride the goddamn range like you did when you were a kid playin Cowboys and Niggers, or Wetbacks, or whatever you shitheads played out here. Now *ride!*

(*Extremely self-consciously,* STEPHEN *begins to ride the range.*)

Slap leather! You're Red Ryder and you're chasin a black hat across the desert out there. Now, go get him!

(STEPHEN *slaps leather and rides the range a little harder.*)

Sound effects!

(STEPHEN *adds weak sound effects—clicks and calls to his horse.*)

What was goddamn Red Ryder's horse's name, Jim?

RICHARD: I don't remember.

TEDDY: Thunder or Midnight, I think. (*To* STEPHEN.) Your horse is Thunder or Midnight—pick one. That giddyap shit's no good anymore.

(STEPHEN *clicks and calls to his horse, calling him Midnight.*)

Stop! . . . Okay, now ride up to the counter and dismount and tie your horse up.

(STEPHEN *does.*)

Bad. Very bad. Okay, now, ya go into this here cafe here, see, and Sweet Cheeks is your only beloved—cause you're Red Ryder and you only got one truly beloved. I mean, as far as I can see, you just don't mess around on the side. But, unlike the homosexual fruit Lone Ranger, you do got yourself this one fine gal here. A great time it was, Jim, when we didn't know enough to wonder at all those vir-ile lads runnin around in weird couples. It's no wonder our generation despises women. All right now, Sweet Nubs, you come on down here and when Red comes in off the range, you say, Red honey, welcome home! Got that?

(*Slowly* ANGEL *moves down the counter to her position, nods assent.*)

Okay, Red, get back there and come *gallopin* up this time, tie up ole Thunder or Midnight, and swagger into the cafe.

(STEPHEN *rides up again, dismounts, and ties up his horse. He starts toward the counter.*)

Swagger!

(STEPHEN *does something of a swagger.*)

ANGEL: Red honey, wel—

TEDDY: Not yet, for chrissake. Let him get in the door . . . smack some dust from his britches.

(STEPHEN *slaps some dust from himself, his eyes on the floor.* ANGEL *looks to* TEDDY *for a signal. He gives it.*)

ANGEL: Red honey, welcome home.

(STEPHEN *stands, his eyes on the floor.*)

TEDDY: Kiss her, Red, for chrissake. Where're your manners, ya schmuck? Pucker up, dumplin.

(STEPHEN *leans across the counter.* ANGEL *presents her face forward, but he kisses her on the cheek.*)

Shit—*cut!* . . . Okay, Red, get over there. Sweet Cheeks, back off. Our Lady of the Violin, com'ere, I got somethin for you to do.

(CLARISSE *looks to* RICHARD.)

Don't look at him like he's gonna give ya permission. This ain't the school dance, honey. If I call cutsees then we got cutsees. Now get behind the counter and when I ride up, you say, Red honey, welcome home! . . . Move!

(CLARISSE *doesn't move . . . .* TEDDY *walks toward them, then suddenly snatches up the violin case.*)

CLARISSE: Don't. Be careful. Please.

(TEDDY *opens the case and then suddenly, carelessly whips out the violin.*)

All right.

(CLARISSE *moves behind the counter.*)

RICHARD: Don't kiss her!

TEDDY: (*Pause; staring at* RICHARD *as if he adores the idiocy of what* RICHARD *chose to say, sharing his reaction with* STEPHEN, *then turning to* CLARISSE.) At two minutes to curtain the female star is taken suddenly by a mysterious illness and you, the prop girl, are thrust into the part. Don't blow it. (*To* STEPHEN *and* ANGEL.) Now, Red, Nubs, watch this, cause this the way I want it.

(*Carrying the violin under his arm,* TEDDY *slaps leather around the diner, whipping his horse on, calling to it. He gallops up to the counter, leaps off his horse, throws the reins over the rail and grandly ties them, swaggers into the cafe, and slaps some dust from his britches.*)

CLARISSE: *(In a monotone.)* Red honey, welcome home.

(TEDDY leans across the counter but CLARISSE has her head turned toward RICHARD. TEDDY grabs her through her pullover by her brassiere, twists the brassiere, and yanks her toward him. RICHARD comes for TEDDY. TEDDY raises the violin over his head as if he would smash it on the counter. RICHARD stops, slowly sits. TEDDY stares at him a moment, then still holding the violin over his head, he leans in to kiss CLARISSE. She turns her face away. He lowers the violin to her turned cheek and turns her mouth to his. He kisses her, after several moments releasing her brassiere. For several moments longer her mouth remains with his. Then she breaks. They stare at each other. TEDDY turns away, seemingly affected. Pause.)

TEDDY: Thanks, Jim, take her away.

CLARISSE: Give me my violin.

TEDDY: Only if you promise to play us some background music.

CLARISSE: All right. Give it to me.

(TEDDY picks up a fork from the counter and tosses it on a tray.)

TEDDY: On those. First a little range-ridin music, then somethin soft and ro-mantic. Play nice and when today's shootin schedule's finished—no pun intended, Jim—you'll get your instrument back. All right, Red, show me somethin, boy.

STEPHEN: *(Pause.)* I don't wanna kiss her.

TEDDY: What's the matter, boy—you queer?

STEPHEN: I just don't wanna kiss her.

TEDDY: Cause she's fat?

STEPHEN: I just don't wanna.

TEDDY: Don't you know what it'd mean to her if you—

STEPHEN: I don't wanna.

TEDDY: Shut up! Don't you understand, boy, that you've got to learn to see yourself in relation to other people's needs. You think I enjoy this work?

85

STEPHEN: I just don't wanna kiss her.

TEDDY: Jesus Christ, I say something of consequence to you, and you give me back "I don't wanna" for the fourth time. I think you're queer, boy, that's what I think.

STEPHEN: I don't care what you think.

(TEDDY has his arm draped across STEPHEN's shoulders. He suddenly tightens his arm around STEPHEN's neck.)

TEDDY: Please care what I think. Okay? *(Pause; STEPHEN nods.)* Now you either do this scene the way I wrote it or I'm gonna make you kiss me. You wanna kiss me?

STEPHEN: *(Straining in the headlock.)* Uh-uh.

TEDDY: Then, boy, play the scene the way I wrote it. There can only be one writer on these films, otherwise the thematic core of the thing gets screwed up. Surely a man's made as many movin pictures as you knows that. *(TEDDY releases STEPHEN.)* The orchestra's tunin up. Okay . . . *hit it.*

(TEDDY sets the action and "music" going. STEPHEN plays the scene as TEDDY called it, though with a marked lessening of intensity from TEDDY's playing of it. CLARISSE accompanies him on fork and tray. STEPHEN swaggers up to the counter. TEDDY signals CLARISSE to cut the music.)

ANGEL: Red honey, welcome home!

TEDDY: Good. Now music!

(CLARISSE slows her rhythm as STEPHEN leans across the counter to kiss ANGEL, who at the moment of contact turns away. CLARISSE, disgusted as much with her own participation as anything, moves down the counter.)

TEDDY: *(To STEPHEN.)* Boy, I don't care *how* big you are over at Metro, this is the last picture *I'm* ever gonna use you in.

(TEDDY turns up stage, somehow disturbed. Pause. To ANGEL:)

Sweet Cheeks, what can I say?

ANGEL: Nothin.

TEDDY: You want this boy to make love to you?

ANGEL: No!

TEDDY: Sure you do. *(To* STEPHEN.*)* You ever been to bed with a woman, Red? *(Nothing from* STEPHEN.*)* I'm talkin to you, boy.

STEPHEN: Yeah.

TEDDY: Bullshit. Well, this woman wants you to make love to her and, by jingo, she's gonna have her way. *(Slapping the counter.)* Right here.

ANGEL: No!

TEDDY: Our Lady, you'll accompany the action of course. Now here's the way we're gonna play it. Red, you'll say to Nubs here that you're goin away and she'll ask ya, Why ya goin away, Red Ryder?—and you'll say, I don't know, cause you're Red Ryder and you don't know a goddamn thing unless someone tells ya—and that's a great way to be, wouldn't you say, Jim? Memmer how it used to be? Oh yeah, none a this horseshit you're into, boy, about re-spon-sibility and ex-i-stential choice. All's the ole Red Ryder knew is he got sealed orders to go away, so he was goin; and so you'll say, I don't know why I'm goin away; and she'll say, Is it because of me?; and you'll say, I don't know if it's because of you—because no one told ya whether that's it or not; and she'll say, I have to know why; and all's you'll be able to say is, I don't know. Say it!

STEPHEN: I don't know.

TEDDY: *(Showing him how.)* I don't know.

STEPHEN: I don't know.

TEDDY: And then, Sweet Cheeks, you'll say, When you comin back, Red Ryder, and whudduyou say, Red?

STEPHEN: I don't know.

TEDDY: *(Pause.)* Uh-uh, no, that's wrong. Because at this juncture, some unknown but officious individual steps to your

ear and whispers: Never. You ain't never comin back, Red
Ryder. And you say to your little dumplin here: I ain't
never comin back. And Nubs here's eyes fill up and she says,
Make love to me then, Ryder, before ya go; and you, bless
ya, Red, you say, We ain't married, Missy Nubs, it
wouldn't be right. I couldn't! I mustn't! *(Pause; then exploding out of himself at something deep and distant.)*
Goddamn it! (Turning on RICHARD.) You a Dodger fan, Jim?

RICHARD: *(Startled.)* No.

TEDDY: *(To* STEPHEN.) *Base*ball! Game grown men used to play
when Jim and me was boys and you weren't the only Red
Ryder around. Who'd ya root for, Jamie?

RICHARD: *(Unsettled.)* Yankees.

TEDDY: *(Laughing distantly.)* You shitbrick. Yeah—we ain't
gonna forget Roger Maris' flattop overnight, are we? Ya
stick with 'em when you moved west, Jimmy? I'll tell ya
what happened to me: When they moved the Duker outta
Brooklyn and into that friggin L.A. Coliseum, they ruined
the career of the only man I ever loved. I'm talkin to you,
Jimble. You speak to that!

RICHARD: I . . . lost interest when they traded Maris, and
Mantle retired.

TEDDY: The Micker, Jesus. Yeah—yeah, maybe that was the end
of it. And that goddamn Yogi Berra. Jesus, I hated that little
bastard. What'd they used to call him?

RICHARD: Mr. Clutch.

TEDDY: Mr. Clutch, my ass.

RICHARD: The Dodgers were losers. You belong together.

TEDDY: Don't you ever imply in my presence that the Duke was
a loser. *(Laughing distantly.)* Ah, the Duker. Edward
Donald Snider, friends, the Duke of Flatbush, pokin 'em
into Bedford Ave. *(Pause; turning on* STEPHEN.) Oh there
was another time, boy, I know it. . . .

(Caught deep inside himself, TEDDY *stops, retreats. Staring at* STEPHEN's *tattoo.)*

Yeah. But that was yesteryear and this is today, and there aint' nothin today to say that a coupla nice kids can't throw each other a nice fuck on a countertop in a diner in New Mexico if they want to. So . . . Mr. Red Ryder and Miss Angel Sweet Nubs, front and center, please and dis-robe.

RICHARD: *(Rising.)* Edwin! It's Ed*win*, not Edward! *Edwin Donald Snider!* Now stop degrading them! We are living in the present and if you—

TEDDY: *Do you* think this woman is impressed by all of your gratuitous bravado? *(To* CLARISSE.*)* Are you? Are you impressed? *(To* RICHARD.*)* Don't you understand there have been landmark discoveries in the fields of apology and psychology suggesting that there is more to manliness and husbandry than pretending willingness to do battle with men you cannot compete with?

*(*TEDDY *stares at* RICHARD.*)*

Hey, Red, how bout Our Lady of the Violin? Like to make love to her?

CLARISSE: *Don't touch me!*

TEDDY: Whudduya say to that, Red? Your first sexual experience of a complete nature with a concert violinist who's not at all unattractive for a woman creeping death-quick into middle age. Maybe she'll even put the fiddle down while y'all consummate.

(Pause.)

Red boy, goddamn it, I'm talkin to you.

STEPHEN: I don't want to.

TEDDY: I swear to God, boy, I think you're queer as a three dollar bill.

STEPHEN: You're a queer!

TEDDY: *(Furiously.) Rise to the occasion, boy! Rise! Rise to it! (Pause.)*

89

Now look at it this way, Red. On the one hand, you got Sweet Cheeks here, untouched by human hands—correct me if I'm wrong, Cheeks. . . . Cheeks? *(Quietly.)* Yeah—untouched. And then, on the other hand, you've got Our Lady of the Violin . . . who's been around.

CLARISSE: You are an obscenity.

TEDDY: And you, madame, hiding behind your instrument and your paucity of word and deed, are a deceitful woman.

(He stares into CLARISSE.)

Hey, Jim, the little woman ever treat you as good as she does this violin you're payin for?

CLARISSE: You stinking filth. You rotten, stinking filth.

RICHARD: Clarisse, stay out of this—

CLARISSE: You come in here and you treat us as though we were somehow truly without worth, as if we were truly no more than dirt. But no, it's not us, it's not us. It's *you*—

RICHARD: All right, Clarisse—

CLARISSE: I know you and I'm not impressed. I *know* you and I want you *out* of here—

RICHARD: *(With a small self-conscious laugh.)* Sshhh, it's all right.

CLARISSE: It's not all right. Don't tell me it's all right—

RICHARD: Don't demean yourself by—

CLARISSE: Don't you talk to me about demeaning myself. This mass of filth walks into our lives and you let him humiliate you beyond all pretense—

RICHARD: He hasn't humiliated me, Clarisse—

CLARISSE: Who gives a good goddamn about . . . *Ed*ward *Sch*neider when the little dignity that remains to you is being reduced—

RICHARD: He hasn't done anything to me but put a hole in my arm!

90

CLARISSE: You'd let him have intercourse with me on the counter if he really wanted to, do you know that?—

RICHARD: Don't be ridiculous!

CLARISSE: What would you do?

RICHARD: I'd do something!

CLARISSE: *You wouldn't stop him because you can't!*

RICHARD: *I'd stop him!*

CLARISSE: *(To* TEDDY.*)* All right, filth, come on, let's see if he can—

RICHARD: *Stop it! Do you understand me? You're making fools of us. You're embarrassing me.*

CLARISSE: *Richard, I am not your added appendage.*

RICHARD: I told you to stay out of this! Now you sit down and pull yourself together—

CLARISSE: *Haven't I been there?* I'm in trouble too, Richard, and I don't trust you anymore.

(Silence. They stare at each other, having gone too far and fixed on the wrong thing in the wrong place and time. RICHARD *suddenly bolts away.* CLARISSE *stands, frozen, for some seconds, then she takes several steps toward* RICHARD *but stops well short of him.)*

TEDDY: This one's dedicated to the Ethredges, y'all.

(He strikes one of the strings of the violin. Pause.)

Hey!—what is this? I thought we came here to dance.

(Pause; quietly.)

Let's dance.

(He drops a quarter into the jukebox and arbitrarily punches three selections. CHERYL *and* LYLE *enter.)*

Get the van fixed?

LYLE: All set.

*(*LYLE *hands* TEDDY *two rolls of friction tape.)*

91

TEDDY: This is the last dance then, gang. Time's gone and I'm gonna ride off into the sunrise.

(A slow ballad comes on.)

Come on, Red, one last memory. You and Nubs lead it off. Get out here, dumplin.

(ANGEL comes out from behind the counter. She has been crying since the ETHREDGES exploded at each other.)

What're ya bawlin about, Cheeks? My God, darlin, be jubilant. Red! Get your ass over to her.

(STEPHEN takes ANGEL loosely by the wrists and begins to do a little two-step shuffle.)

(Accentless.) Mrs. Ethredge, I believe this is my dance.

(CLARISSE holds, glances at RICHARD.)

RICHARD: The man's waiting to dance with you.

(TEDDY hands the violin to RICHARD.)

TEDDY: You get the violin, Jim.

(RICHARD takes the violin, looks at it a moment, then places it on the table. RICHARD and CLARISSE stare at each other a moment. TEDDY lifts a hand toward CLARISSE. She glances at the violin and moves to him. He touches her face. She stares with simple defiance at him.)

My darlin, I love your style.

(He smiles at her, then seems almost to laugh at her. He takes her to him and begins to dance her around. He gets a look at ANGEL and STEPHEN.)

Jesus, Red, if you and Sweet Cheeks don't make a picture to warm the heart, I don't know what does.

(CLARISSE's free arm hangs at her side. TEDDY slaps it up around his neck. For a moment she leaves her hand on him, then thrusts it back to her side. TEDDY stops dancing, looks into her face.)

Memmer, my darlin, when we used to do it thisaway?

(He digs his fingers into her buttocks, pressing her to his groin with such force that his arms quiver slightly. She slowly exerts herself against his strength and slowly he allows her to break from him. She stares at him again with that simple look of defiance.)

All right, Red, break! You and Cheeks pick new partners.

(ANGEL and STEPHEN break but neither moves.)

Pick a new partner, Nubs. Move it, darlin.

(ANGEL turns slowly toward LYLE.)

ANGEL: Wanna dance, Lyle?

LYLE: 'Fraid I'm not much for dancin with this thing. *(Indicating his brace.)*

TEDDY: Sure ya are. Why there's crippled folks in bowlin leagues.

LYLE: I wish you wouldn't ask me to do this.

TEDDY: I fail to see, sir, that you have the right to any dispensations the others don't. Do it.

(LYLE and ANGEL begin to dance after a fashion.)

Red, what're you doin standin around with your thumb up your ass. You see Cheryl standin there like a goddamn wallflower.

STEPHEN: *(To CHERYL.)* You wanna dance?

CHERYL: No.

STEPHEN: *(To TEDDY.)* She don't want to.

CHERYL: Teddy, the car's ready. It's enough.

TEDDY: I'll say when it's enough. Dance with goddamn Red Ryder.

CHERYL: I don't want to dance, Teddy. I wanna get out of here.

TEDDY: And I want you to dance with this boy.

CHERYL: I'm not one of them, damn it, I'm with you.

TEDDY: So what, darlin? Were you under the misapprehension that makes you privileged? . . . Well, it don't. Uh-uh. No—you functional too, darlin. Nothin else really. *(Quietly.)* Now you dance.

(She shakes her head.)

(Absolutely firmly.) You gotta dance, sweetheart.

(She moves toward STEPHEN. TEDDY steps to her, holds out his hand. Slowly she passes him the gun.)

(To STEPHEN.) You keep your eyes off her breasts, boy. Okay?

(STEPHEN and CHERYL begin to dance. TEDDY heads for RICHARD.)

RICHARD: Stay away from me!

TEDDY: You dance with her, you sorry son of a bitch. The committee put a lotta plannin into this social.

(CLARISSE reaches for RICHARD. He throws her hand off and moves onto the dance floor. He stands with CLARISSE but does not dance, her hand unheld on his palm.)

All right, everybody dance!

(TEDDY stamps his foot and claps with the music, his stamping and clapping becoming maniacal. Suddenly he leaps at RICHARD and CLARISSE and spins them round and round, screaming at them:)

DANCE! DANCE! GODDAMN IT, DANCE!

(He derives no satisfaction from this and now throws RICHARD to the floor and against CLARISSE's cries of resistance, he clamps her arms above her head, peels her pullover up over her head, and yanks her brassiere up, exposing her breasts. He bears her blindly to STEPHEN:)

THERE, BOY, TITS! TITS!

(And now across to LYLE who backs away as if bitten.)

THERE, OLE MAN, TITS!

94

(TEDDY *thrusts* CLARISSE *away from him and slumps against the counter.* RICHARD *has risen by now and reached* TEDDY. *As he grips* TEDDY's *shoulder from the rear,* TEDDY *rifles his elbow into* RICHARD's *stomach, turns and kicks* RICHARD *in the groin.* RICHARD *drops like a sack of cement.* TEDDY *is panting. He looks about him a moment, then with an animal cry he tears the jukebox plug from its socket. The music winds to a stop, the lights go out on the machine.* CLARISSE *moves down to* RICHARD, *touches him.*)

RICHARD: *Don't touch me!* Please . . . don't touch me.

(TEDDY *pants, stares wildly into space. He finally snaps his eyes to* STEPHEN, *says distantly:*)

TEDDY: Red Ryder . . .

(*He snaps up the two rolls of friction tape. He goes behind the counter and gets a large French knife and a small paring knife.*)

Okay, Red Ryder, start taping hands behind backs and feet and make them tight or I'll cut your pecker off, if you've got one.

(*He throws a roll of tape to* STEPHEN.)

Start with Sweet Cheeks. If her hands are taped, she can't touch you with them.

(STEPHEN *moves to* ANGEL.)

Get some food together, Cheryl.

(CHERYL *does not move.*)

Punishin me, darlin?

(TEDDY *comes out from behind the counter with the knives.*)

Gentleman Jim next. (*To* CLARISSE.) Get the big offenders first, huh?

(STEPHEN *is waiting for something to cut* ANGEL's *tape with.* TEDDY *slides the paring knife over to him.* STEPHEN *picks it up, holds it, looks to* TEDDY.)

One last gesture for the Old West?

(TEDDY snort-laughs at STEPHEN.)

Get on with it, boy.

(STEPHEN gets on with it.)

LYLE: You don't have to tape me, son.

TEDDY: What in the hell's the matter with you, ole man? Tape him up!

(STEPHEN moves on to LYLE. TEDDY finishes taping RICHARD by drawing his taped legs up to his taped hands and taping those together.)

Here's the final ignominy, Jim: to be trussed up like a butchered hog and left on display. *(To LYLE.)* Somehow, you old buzzard, with your tit sucking eyes and your ass kissing demeanor, you make me just as sick as the rest of us do.

(STEPHEN does LYLE's feet, then ANGEL's. TEDDY moves CLARISSE to the opposite side of the diner, sits her down. He takes the two-inch adhesive tape that was used earlier to bind RICHARD's wound and tears off a strip.)

Red Ryder—

(STEPHEN looks around and TEDDY throws him the roll of adhesive tape.)

—mouths.

(TEDDY tapes CLARISSE's hands behind her back. He comes around to tape her feet.)

Yeah, Jim, the truth of the thing is that there do gotta be somethin beyond the Cadillac. Ya know what I mean, Jim?

(Pause.)

(To CLARISSE.) And beyond the violin. Don't there, darlin?

(CLARISSE says nothing; but then, she doesn't have to.)

Yeah . . . well, if I took that away from you . . . I'm sorry.

CLARISSE: Are you?

(They stare at each other.)

TEDDY: No. But I wish I were.

(Hurriedly he presses the adhesive tape to her mouth. STEPHEN *has finished his work and is standing at the counter.* TEDDY *turns to him.)*

I want one more thing from you, Red. I want you to take this knife . . .

(He slams the French knife into the countertop.)

. . . and I want you to cut that tattoo out of your arm. Then I want you to hand it to me to take with me.

(He stares at STEPHEN. *Silence.)*

Ah, Stephen. Ah, Stevie, you despicable chickenshit.

*(*TEDDY *turns from* STEPHEN *in disgust, moves toward the roll of adhesive tape which* STEPHEN *left downstage beside* ANGEL. *As he does,* STEPHEN *yanks the French knife out of the counter, screams his insides long and open, and rushes with deadly earnestness at* TEDDY's *belly.* TEDDY *catches* STEPHEN's *wrists, heaves him backward onto the floor, and draws and cocks the revolver. He presses the revolver's muzzle into* STEPHEN's *face.)*

CHERYL: *Teddy!*

TEDDY: Red honey, welcome home.

*(*TEDDY *straddles* STEPHEN, *presses the gun against* STEPHEN's *eye.)*

It's no good anymore, boy. It's too late. I thought if anyone understood that, you did.

(A long pause, then TEDDY *releases the revolver's hammer.)*

But your sentence ain't to die, Red Ryder. It's to live, looking back on that inept charge across this room as the high spot of your life's prime. . . . Now roll over and put your hands behind your back.

*(*STEPHEN *rolls over and* TEDDY *tapes him. Meanwhile:)*

Clean out Gentleman Jim's pockets, Cheryl.

CHERYL: Teddy, we're in so much trouble.

TEDDY: Yeah. Well, you can stay if you want. Take your chances. It doesn't make any difference to me. *(To* LYLE.*)* Think you can save her, ole man? Huh? What kinda game plan you give her for her salvation? *(To* CHERYL.*)* Some choice you got, sweetheart.

*(*CHERYL *looks from* LYLE *to* TEDDY, *holds on* TEDDY *a moment, then goes listlessly to* RICHARD *and begins to go through his pockets.)*

How long's it been since you had a woman, ole man?

*(*LYLE *doesn't answer.)*

How bout that, sweetheart? Here ya got Mr. Striker, who can't remember the last time he had a woman; Red, who ain't never had one; and Sweet Nubs, who ain't never really been kissed. My God, love, you could become a regular welfare organization around here. Except that would be just one more roll of blubber for you, wouldn't it, Nubs, this tight little girl with her fine, pointed breasts comin between you and Mr. Striker.

(Pause. He turns on LYLE.*)*

Ah, Mr. Striker.

(He turns to CHERYL.*)*

Get some food together.

*(*TEDDY *sits at the counter and strips* RICHARD's *wallet.* CHERYL *gets together several small boxes of Wheaties and other cereal, some sandwich meat and a loaf of bread.)*

Breakfast of Champions. That where it all started to go bad, ya think, Jim? The Reverend Bob Richards polevaulting into our churches and hearts for . . . *Wheaties!* Gonna have this bronzed and send it back to you and Red. *(To* CHERYL.*)* You ready, sweetheart?

CHERYL: *(Pause.)* I'm not going with you, Teddy.

*(*TEDDY *looks at her for several seconds, then goes for his*

fatigue jacket. That on, he tears the receiver out of the phone, gathers up his food, stares at CLARISSE *a moment, and then moves down to* STEPHEN.)

TEDDY: When you comin back, Red Ryder? (*Nothing from* STEPHEN.)

Tell me one last time, boy. . . . Tell me!

STEPHEN: Never.

(TEDDY *slaps a piece of tape across* STEPHEN's *mouth, dumps the revolver into the bread sack, and exits without a look at anyone.*)

(*Silence.* CHERYL *seems frozen for some seconds, then she moves to the edge of the counter. She is not quite able to make her decision. She comes tentatively out from behind the counter. She stares across the others, fixes on* LYLE, *takes several steps toward him. Then she hears someone coming and retreats behind the counter, pressing herself to the wall.*)

(CLARK *enters at his own busy pace.*)

CLARK: What in *the* hell!

(*After a cursory glance around he makes for the cash register, much surprised to find the money still in the register.*)

What in the name of sweet Jesus! (*Taking* CHERYL *in.*) What the hell're *you* doin?

(CHERYL *does not move.* CLARK *whips out his pocketknife and bends over* STEPHEN. *He yanks the tape off* STEPHEN's *mouth.*)

STEPHEN: Ouch! Christ!

CLARK: What the hell happened?

STEPHEN: What the hell's it look like?

CLARK: (*Freeing* STEPHEN's *hands and feet.*) Don't smart mouth me, Red. It looks like someone held ya up and didn't take nothin is what it looks like. (*Moving to* ANGEL; *indicating* CHERYL.) Who's she? (*To* STEPHEN, *who has lighted a cig-*

arette at the counter.) Don't just stand there, boy, lend a hand. *(To* ANGEL.*)* They didn't take *nothin?*

ANGEL: Just some bread and sandwich meat and some cereal—

CLARK: How much?

ANGEL: He shot that man.

CLARK: Huh!

(CLARK hurries to RICHARD, begins to free him.)

How bad he get ya, neighbor?

ANGEL: Ya gotta take the tape off his mouth before he can talk.

(CLARK glances irritably at ANGEL, then carefully removes the tape from RICHARD's mouth, as if he might be wounded there.)

CLARK: Easy does it here...

RICHARD: Call the sheriff. I'm all right. Call the sheriff and don't let that girl out of here.

CLARK: *(Starting for the phone.)* She ain't goin nowhere—

(He sees the receiver has been ripped out.)

S'ome bitch!

(He turns to LYLE, whom STEPHEN has freed.)

Get over to your station and get a hold of the Highway Police and that goddamn Garcia.

LYLE: *(Indicating CHERYL.)* What about her?

RICHARD: *(Infuriated.)* What do you mean, what about her? She's going to be prosecuted, that's what about her!

LYLE: I got the license number, Tommy. He's headin for Mexico and he's got a loada dope.

CLARK: Time's short now. Move on, Lyle. He get across that border and the goddamn Mex's'll set him up in a hotel somewheres. Vamanos! Chop chop!

LYLE: Tommy, about this girl here—

RICHARD: Hold it! He's taking a load of dope *into* Mexico? You don't take dope *into* Mexico. You take it *out.* He's heading back to California. *(To* CHERYL.*)* Is that right?

*(*CHERYL *does not move.* RICHARD *drags her out from behind the counter and screams in her face.)*

Is that right?

*(*CHERYL *looks to* LYLE.*)*

LYLE: Ya better tell him, miss.

CHERYL: *(Pause.)* Yes.

RICHARD: San Diego?

(Pause. CHERYL *nods.)*

LYLE: I'll tell 'em.

*(*LYLE *hustles off while* RICHARD *is thrusting* CHERYL *onto a stool.* RICHARD *turns after him too late.)*

RICHARD: Hold it! Hold it . . .! *(Turning to* CLARK.*)* I don't trust that man.

CLARK: Say now, neighbor, Lyle Striker's as trustworthy a man as ever's been my pleasure to know.

RICHARD: Really?

CLARK: Don't you worry yourself none—we'll get this fella.

RICHARD: I'm not worried.

CLARK: *(To* STEPHEN.*)* Three men here and one fella did this?

ANGEL: He had a gun.

CLARK: *(Ignoring her.)* And what'd you do, Redbird? Just sit here on your butt drinkin up my coffee and greasin up the customer newspaper?

STEPHEN: *(Powerfully.)* Up your hole, Clark, with a ten foot pole.

ANGEL: Stephen tried to do somethin. He—

CLARK: All right, boy, that's all for you. You're as of here and now fired. *(Turning to* ANGEL.*)* You sure that's all he took?

RICHARD: He took some money from me. About a hundred and seventy dollars.

CLARK: (*Turning back to* STEPHEN, *ignoring* RICHARD.) To tell ya the honest to God truth, boy, after that by-pass open, I wanted to shut down at night, but cause a your momma, I kept you on and I stayed open, to the detriment of my nearly major source of income.

STEPHEN: You're a goddamn charity organization, Clark, no question about it.

CLARK: Boy, somebody oughta wash your mouth out with lye soap.

STEPHEN: (*Stepping up to* CLARK, *face to face.*) Yeah, and I suppose you're the one's gonna try it.

RICHARD: Why don't you both *shut up!*

CLARK: Say now, neighbor—

RICHARD: *Shut up!*

CLARISSE: Richard . . .

RICHARD: And why don't you shut up too!

(RICHARD *suddenly leaps at her violin, takes it up like a bat and flies across the room, evidently intent on smashing it against the opposite table.* STEPHEN *throws himself toward* RICHARD, *meets him, and the two of them become a piece of still statuary holding a violin above their heads and staring into each other's eyes. They hold unmoving for several seconds before* STEPHEN *tries to say "I don't know why I did that," but says only:*)

STEPHEN: I . . . (*Pause.*) . . . I'm . . .

(*—and slowly takes the violin from* RICHARD's *hands, holds it gently, and returns it to its case.* LYLE *enters.*)

LYLE: Got the Highway Police out after him. I told 'em ya had to be in New Orleans and they said you'd have to come on down to the station and sign some papers first. I told 'em you was shot a little. They'll have a doctor there.

RICHARD: Very philanthropic. (*Indicating* CHERYL.) What did they say to do with her?

(LYLE *says nothing; he obviously said nothing to the State Police about her.* RICHARD *laughs a sardonic and incredulous laugh.*)

Surely you're not *serious*.

(*He stares at* LYLE, *the laugh dead on his face. He turns to* CLARK.)

Can you take this girl and lead us to the police?

CLARK: S'pose so.

RICHARD: Oh, I wouldn't want to put you *out*. Any of you! I'd hate to insist on any adherence to the *law*.

CLARK: Don't you worry none about adherence to the law. We adhere plenty.

RICHARD: All right then, let's *go*. Clarisse.

CLARK: (*To* ANGEL.) You get on that chile sauce. I be back to check the books in a while.

STEPHEN: Hey!

(*Everyone stops.*)

(*To* CLARISSE.) Take me as far as Baton Rouge?

RICHARD: I wouldn't take you as far as the front door.

STEPHEN: (*To* CLARISSE.) Will ya?

RICHARD: (*Laughing sourly.*) Why are you asking her?

CLARISSE: You don't have your clothing, your—

STEPHEN: I'm ready to go just like I am. Gimme my pay, Clark.

CLARK: What's your momma gonna say, boy?

(*There is a sting in that, but* STEPHEN *moves to* LYLE, *digs out a small roll of bills.*)

STEPHEN: (*Privately, to* LYLE.) Here's forty bucks. You lend me thirty-five and you buy her that car at Potter's for me. You wanna do that for me still?

LYLE: *(Pause; he glances at* ANGEL.*)* Sure, Red.

STEPHEN: Just tell her I'm goin to Baton Rouge and when I get settled in I'll write.

LYLE: Son, shouldn't you check in with Mizzes Williams first?

STEPHEN: *(To* CLARISSE.*)* You gonna gimme a hitch?

RICHARD: No, I'm sorry.

CLARISSE: We'll take you.

(She turns to RICHARD.*)*

We'll take him as far as Baton Rouge.

RICHARD: I'm not at all sure I'm going on to New Orleans.

CLARISSE: *(Pause.)* Then I'll take him. I'd like you to come with me . . . but if you can't . . . *(She shrugs, not offensively, only simply.)* all right.

RICHARD: Look—let's go down to the police station.

*(*CLARISSE *nods to* STEPHEN *as* RICHARD *moves to the door. They exit.)*

STEPHEN: *(To* CLARK.*)* Gimme my pay.

*(*CLARK *carefully peels off* STEPHEN'*s salary.* STEPHEN *snaps it from him.)*

All right—now the next time you talk to ole man Foster, you tell him for me that he can take this whole entire diner and ram it up his rosy red rectum. You tell him that for me, will ya?

CLARK: I'll be sure to tell him, Red.

STEPHEN: Yeah, you tell him that for me and I'll appreciate it. And then you tell him when he's got that digested real good in his intestines that he should ram you right up there after it.

*(*STEPHEN, *a smile almost attacking his mouth, nods to* ANGEL, *heads behind the counter to get his stuff together.* CLARK *fires daggers after him, then grabs* CHERYL *and moves to* LYLE. *He looks at* LYLE *as if* LYLE *and he are somehow*

in it together against STEPHEN, *is about to say something, doesn't, and throws off at* ANGEL.)

CLARK: I be back. *(He exits, pushing* CHERYL *ahead of him.)* I be back.

*(*STEPHEN *comes out from behind the counter with his carton of Raleighs and a current* PLAYBOY *magazine. He goes to his stool, smiling at* LYLE *and* ANGEL *as if he has just conquered the world. He stuffs his pockets with his pack of cigarettes and his matches, snaps up a lightweight flannel shirt, and heads for the door.)*

ANGEL: Stephen!—

*(*STEPHEN *stops between* LYLE *and* ANGEL.)*

(Pause.) You take care of yourself now. Okay?

*(*STEPHEN *doesn't know what to do, though he knows he must do something.)*

STEPHEN: Don't you worry about ole Number One here.

(He walks self-consciously over to her and in lieu of kissing or hugging her, he kind of mushes her with both hands on the shoulder and tells her:)

You just worry about your own self.

(Pause. Then he crosses to LYLE, *stops, gives* LYLE *a little elbow in the chest.)*

So long, suckers.

(And exits.)

ANGEL: G'bye.

*(*LYLE *looks at her but she can't look at him. He starts toward her; as he gets close,* ANGEL *moves away from him and back behind the counter. Silence.)*

LYLE: It's good. He'll be better off.

ANGEL: *(Nodding vigorously.)* Oh—I agree.

LYLE: Yep, got himself a real good future in stock if he can get goin with Mizzes Williams.

ANGEL: I'll bet it's a real nice place she's got.

LYLE: Oh yeah—no doubt about that. Ya don't have a restaurant in Baton Rouge where the help wears tuxedos less'n you're runnin a high class establishment.

ANGEL: I'll say.

(Silence.)

LYLE: Welp, guess I better get to cleanin some rooms.

(Pause.)

Comin over for T.V. tonight? Sunday. Got "Bonanza."

ANGEL: Oh—gee, I don't think so, Lyle. I think . . . My mom and me, we had a extra special good one this mornin. Maybe I oughta just go on home and spend the evenin with her and gra'ma.

LYLE: Sure. Sure. No need to explain. *(Pause.)* Maybe tomorrow night.

(ANGEL smiles thinly.)

You know you're welcome anytime, kid. Any-time.

ANGEL: Car just pulled into the station.

LYLE: Hmm?

ANGEL: A car.

LYLE: Ah.

ANGEL: For gas, it looks like.

LYLE: *(Pause.)* Welp . . . see ya at lunch, kid.

(ANGEL cannot meet his eyes. He stares at her head.)

(Quietly, almost inaudibly.) Okay, okay . . . I'm comin . . .

(He exits. ANGEL looks into space, then around the diner. Pause. She moves to STEPHEN's area, looks at it. She stabs up the remnant of his stale donut. She looks at it, then tears off a small piece of it and puts it in her mouth. She lifts her head, staring toward the window, chewing. The lights fade.)

106